Best Easy Day Hikes
Greensboro and Winston-Salem

Gracias por todo lo que has hecho
Por mí y mi familia. Te lo agradecemos
mucho y te deseamos a ti y tu familia
paz y vida prospera.

CESAR BAHENA
16 MAY 14

Por favor mantente en comunicación
y si llegas a venir al desierto,
MI CASA ES TU CASA.
(760) 702-2165
CESAR_BAHENA@HOTMAIL.COM
69594 NORTHHAMPTON AVE
CATHEDRAL CITY, CA 92234

Help Us Keep This Guide Up to Date

Every effort has been made by the author and editors to make this guide as accurate and useful as possible. However, many things can change after a guide is published—trails are rerouted, regulations change, facilities come under new management, etc.

We would love to hear from you concerning your experiences with this guide and how you feel it could be improved and kept up to date. While we may not be able to respond to all comments and suggestions, we'll take them to heart, and we'll also make certain to share them with the author. Please send your comments and suggestions to the following address:

Globe Pequot Press
Reader Response/Editorial Department
P.O. Box 480
Guilford, CT 06437

Or you may e-mail us at:

editorial@GlobePequot.com

Thanks for your input, and happy trails!

Best Easy Day Hikes Series

Best Easy Day Hikes Greensboro and Winston-Salem

Johnny Molloy

FALCON GUIDES

GUILFORD, CONNECTICUT
HELENA, MONTANA

AN IMPRINT OF GLOBE PEQUOT PRESS

FALCONGUIDES®

Copyright © 2010 by Morris Book Publishing, LLC

FalconGuides is an imprint of Globe Pequot Press, and Falcon, FalconGuides, and Outfit Your Mind are registered trademarks of Morris Book Publishing, LLC.

Project editor: Jessica Haberman
Layout artist: Kevin Mak
Maps: Hartdale Maps © Morris Book Publishing, LLC

TOPO! Explorer software and SuperQuad source maps courtesy of National Geographic Maps. For information about TOPO! Explorer, TOPO!, and Nat Geo Maps products, go to www.topo.com or www.natgeomaps.com.

Library of Congress Cataloging-in-Publication Data
Molloy, Johnny, 1961-
  Best easy day hikes, Greensboro and Winston-Salem / Johnny Molloy.
      p. cm. – (FalconGuides)
  ISBN 978-0-7627-5462-5
  1.   Hiking–North Carolina–Greensboro Region–Guidebooks. 2.   Greensboro Region (N.C.)–Guidebooks. 3.   Hiking–North Carolina–Winston-Salem Region–Guidebooks. 4.   Winston-Salem Region (N.C.)–Guidebooks. I. Title.
  GV199.42.N662G74 2010
  796.5109756–dc22

                                          2009037986

Printed in the United States of America
10 9 8 7 6 5 4 3 2 1

Contents

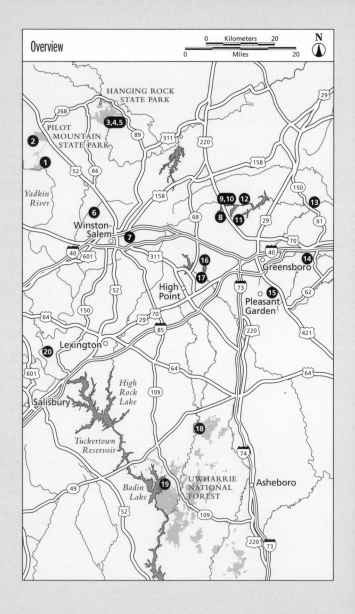

Acknowledgments

Thanks to all the people who helped me with this book, namely Pamela Morgan and also John "Gutsy Performer" Bland. Also, thanks to all the park personnel who answered my tireless questions while trying to manage these jewels of the Piedmont. The biggest thanks go to the hikers of the Triad, for without y'all the trails wouldn't be there in the first place.

Introduction

The cliffs of the ancient peak, today known as Pilot Mountain, offered a southward view that extending into the Triad—Greensboro, Winston-Salem, High Point, as well as surrounding communities. The outspread landscape contained the hikes in this guide. I mentally recounted all the beauty lying within sight. Nearby, the Yadkin River continued carving a valley as it had done for centuries, past Bean Shoals a few miles distant and Boones Cave in Davidson County. To the east the Sauratown Mountains rose from the Piedmont. They offered views from outcrops on Moore's Wall and Hanging Rock and a trip to the geologically fascinating Window Falls.

Greensboro's watershed lakes, north of downtown, held still other hikes that traveled along streams and shoreline. Laurel Bluff Trail climbed a hillside covered in beech trees, eventually leading to an overlook on Lake Townsend. Bur-Mil Park mixed foot trails into Greensboro's extensive greenway system. The hike at Guilford Courthouse National Military Battlefield explored an American Revolutionary site. Triad hikers can go further back in time, exploring the 1750s Moravian community at Bethabara Park in Winston-Salem, using greenways and footpaths that also travel by a tree-studded marshland.

Other destinations were developed purely with recreation in mind. Salem Lake Park created one of the area's early greenways. It circles the impoundment and ties into an expanding greenway system. Northeast Park is one of the area's newest preserves and was laid out with trails in mind, along with ample other facilities. Guilford Mackintosh Park, a watershed lake serving Burlington, was modeled after those in Greensboro and offers a stellar lakeside trek. Hagen-Stone Park is a time-honored favorite park that also offers camping opportunities. A fine trail loops through the many ponds scattered within its bounds. Piedmont Environmental Center, the pride of High Point, delivers two excellent loop hikes situated along the shores of High Point Lake, as well as an environmental education center and a famed large-scale graphic relief map of North Carolina.

I scanned farther south to the Uwharrie Mountains, ancient peaks themselves, softened over millennia and now only extending 1,000 feet high. Yet these mountains, part of the Uwharrie National Forest, held in their grasp the Birkhead Mountains Wilderness, where Triad city residents can enter the back of beyond. Elsewhere in the Uwharries, the Badin Lake Loop gives hikers another opportunity to explore the national forest.

With this guide in hand—and willing feet—you can explore the greater Triad region. No matter where you go, the trails in this guide will enhance your outdoor experience and leave you appreciating the natural splendors of the greater Carolina Piedmont. Enjoy.

The Nature of Greensboro and the Greater Triad

The Triad's hiking grounds range from singletrack mountain paths to trails along bountiful lakes and streams to flat and paved greenways. Hikes in this guide cover the gamut. While by definition a best easy day hike is not strenuous and generally poses little danger to the traveler, knowing a few details about the nature of the Triad will enhance your explorations.

Weather

The Triad certainly experiences all four seasons, though it is a little long on summer. Summer can be very hot and is the least popular hiking season. Thunderstorms can pop up in the afternoons. I recommend hiking during the early morning or late in the evening in summer.

Hiking activity increases when the first northerly fronts of fall sweep cool, clear air across the Piedmont. Crisp mornings give way to warm afternoons. Fall, drier than summer, is the driest of all seasons.

Winter can bring subfreezing days and chilling rains. However, a brisk hiking pace will keep you warm. Each cold month has several days of mild weather.

Spring is more variable. A warm day can be followed by a cold one. Extensive spring rains bring regrowth but also keep hikers indoors. But avid hikers will find more good hiking days than they will have time to hike in spring as in every other season.

Critters

Triad trail treaders will encounter mostly benign creatures on these trails, such as deer, squirrels, rabbits, wild turkeys, and a variety of songbirds. More rarely seen (during the daylight hours especially) are coyotes, raccoons, and opossums. Deer in some of the parks are remarkably tame and may linger on or close to the trail as you approach. If you feel uncomfortable when encountering any critter, keep your distance and they will generally keep theirs.

Be Prepared

Hiking in the greater Triad is generally safe. Still, hikers should be prepared, whether they are out for a short stroll along the Bethabara Greenway or venturing into the secluded Birkhead Mountains Wilderness. Some specific advice:

- Know the basics of first aid, including how to treat bleeding; bites and stings; and fractures, strains, or sprains. Carry a first-aid kit on each excursion.

- Familiarize yourself with the symptoms of heat exhaustion and heat stroke. Heat exhaustion symptoms include heavy sweating, muscle cramps, headache, dizziness, and fainting. Should you or any of your hiking party exhibit any of these symptoms, cool the victim down immediately by rehydrating and getting him or her to an air-conditioned location. Cold showers also help reduce body temperature. Heat stroke is much more serious: The victim may lose consciousness and the skin is hot and dry to the touch. In this event, call 911 immediately.

- Regardless of the weather, your body needs a lot of water while hiking. A full thirty-two-ounce bottle is the minimum for these short hikes, but more is always better. Bring a full water bottle, even if water is available along the trail.

- Don't drink from streams, rivers, creeks, or lakes without first treating or filtering the water. Waterways and water bodies may host a variety of contaminants, including giardia, which can cause serious intestinal unrest.

- Prepare for extremes of both heat and cold by dressing in layers.

- Carry a backpack in which you can store extra clothing; ample drinking water and food; and whatever goodies, like guidebooks, cameras, and binoculars, you might want. Consider bringing a GPS with tracking capabilities.

- Most Triad trails have cell phone coverage. Bring your device, but make sure you've turned it off or got it on the vibrate setting while hiking. There's nothing like a "wake the dead"–loud ring to startle every creature, including fellow hikers.

- Keep children under careful watch. Trails travel along many streams and lakes that are not recommended for swimming. Hazards along some of the trails include poison ivy, uneven footing, and steep drop-offs; make sure children don't stray from the designated route. Children should carry a plastic whistle. If they become lost, they should stay in one place and blow the whistle to summon help.

Zero Impact

Trails in the Triad and neighboring foothills are well used year-round. We, as trail users, must be especially vigilant to make sure our passage leaves no lasting mark. Here are some basic guidelines for preserving trails in the region:

- Pack out all your own trash, including biodegradable items like orange peels. You might also pack out garbage left by less-considerate hikers.

- Don't approach or feed any wild creatures—the ground squirrel eyeing your snack food is best able to survive if it remains self-reliant.

- Don't pick wildflowers or gather rocks, antlers, feathers, and other treasures along the trail. Removing these items will only take away from the next hiker's experience.

- Avoid damaging trailside soils and plants by remaining on the established route. This is also a good rule of thumb for avoiding poison ivy and stinging nettle, common regional trailside irritants.

- Be courteous by not making loud noises while hiking.

- Many of these trails are multiuse, which means you'll share them with other hikers, trail runners, mountain bikers, and equestrians. Familiarize yourself with the proper trail etiquette, yielding the trail when appropriate.

- Use outhouses at trailheads or along the trail.

Triad Area Boundaries and Corridors

For the purposes of this guide, best easy day hikes are confined to a one-hour drive from downtown Greensboro. The hikes reach into Winston-Salem; Burlington; and the counties of Forsyth, Guilford, Montgomery, Davidson, Surry, and Stokes.

A number of major highways and interstates converge in the Triad. Directions to trailheads are given from these arteries, which include I-40 and Business I-40, I-85 and Business I-85, US 52, and US 220.

Land Management

The following government organizations manage most of the public lands described in this guide and can provide further information on these hikes and other trails in their service areas.

- North Carolina State Parks, 1615 MSC, Raleigh 27699; (919) 733-4181; www.ncparks.gov. A complete listing of state parks is available on the Web site, along with park brochures and maps.

- Greensboro Parks & Recreation Department, 1001 Fourth St., Greensboro 27405; (336) 373-2574; www .greensboro-nc.gov/departments/Parks

- Uwharrie National Forest, 789 NC 24/27 East, Troy 27371; (910) 576-6391; www.cs.unca.edu/nfsnc/ recreation/uwharrie

- City of Winston-Salem Recreation & Parks Department, 1001 Salem Lake Rd., Winston-Salem 27106; (336) 727-2063; www.cityofws.org/

How to Use This Guide

This guide is designed to be simple and easy to use. Each hike is described with a map and summary information that delivers the trail's vital statistics, including distance, difficulty, fees and permits, park hours, canine compatibility, and trail contacts. Directions to the trailhead are also provided, along with a general description of what you'll see along the way. A detailed route finder (Miles and Directions) sets forth mileages between significant landmarks along the trail.

Hike Selection

This guide describes trails that are accessible to every hiker, whether visiting from out of town or someone lucky enough to live in the Triad. The hikes are no longer than 7 miles round-trip, and most are considerably shorter. They range in difficulty from flat excursions perfect for a family outing to more challenging treks in the Sauratown and Uwharrie Mountains. While these trails are among the best, keep in mind that nearby trails, often in the same park or preserve, may offer options better suited to your needs. I've sought to space hikes throughout the greater Triad so that wherever your starting point, you'll find a great easy day hike nearby.

Difficulty Ratings

These are all easy hikes, but easy is a relative term. To aid in the selection of a hike that suits particular needs and abilities, each is rated easy, moderate, or more challenging. Bear in mind that even more challenging routes can be made easy by hiking within your limits and taking rests when you need them.

- **Easy** hikes are generally short and flat, taking no longer than an hour to complete.
- **Moderate** hikes involve increased distance and relatively mild changes in elevation; they will take one to two hours to complete.
- **More challenging** hikes feature some steep stretches, greater distances, and generally take longer than two hours to complete.

These are completely subjective ratings—consider that what you think is easy is entirely dependent on your level of fitness and the adequacy of your gear (primarily shoes). If you are hiking with a group, you should select a hike with a rating that's appropriate for the least fit and prepared in your party.

Approximate hiking times are based on the assumption that on flat ground, most walkers average 2 miles per hour. Adjust that rate by the steepness of the terrain and your level of fitness (subtract time if you're an aerobic animal and add time if you're hiking with kids), and you have a ballpark hiking duration. Be sure to add more time if you plan to picnic or take part in other activities like bird watching or photography.

Trail Finder

Best Hikes for River and Stream Lovers

Best Hikes for Lake Lovers

Best Hikes for Children

Best Hikes for Dogs

Best Hikes for Great Views

Best Hikes for Nature Lovers

Best Hikes for History Buffs

Map Legend

══8══	Interstate Highway
══19══	U.S. Highway
══34══	State Highway
═══	Local Road
= = = =	Unpaved Road
▬▬▬▬	Featured Trail
- - - -	Trail
▬▬▬	Paved Trail
·········	Horse Trail
～～	River/Creek
-··-··-	Intermittent Stream
⬚	Local/State Park
▬	National Forest/State Park (Overview)
‖‖‖	Boardwalk
⏝	Bridge
▲	Camping
❷	Information Center
℗	Parking
▲	Peak
🛆	Picnic Area
■	Point of Interest/Structure
🛉	Restroom
○	Town
⓫	Trailhead
◈	Viewpoint/Overlook
≋	Waterfall
⟋	Spring

1 Horne Creek–Yadkin River Loop

This hike travels the intimate Horne Creek valley before meeting an old road that leads down to the Yadkin River. Here, cruise along the big and scenic waterway as it flows past noisy Bean Shoals and the Yadkin River Islands. The return trip takes you over piney hills before returning to the attractive picnic area and trailhead on Horne Creek.

Distance: 4.1-mile loop

Approximate hiking time: 1.5 to 2 hours

Difficulty: Moderate, a few hills

Trail surface: Natural surfaces

Best season: March through May; September through November

Other trail users: Horses on Yadkin Islands Trail

Canine compatibility: Leashed dogs permitted

Fees and permits: No fees or permits required

Schedule: Open 8:00 a.m. to sunset

Maps: USGS Pinnacle and Siloam; Pilot Mountain State Park Hiking Trails; www.ncparks .gov/Visit/parks/pimo/pics/ parkmap.pdf

Trail contact: Pilot Mountain State Park, 1792 Pilot Knob Park Rd., Pinnacle 27043; (336) 325-2355; www.ncparks.gov

Finding the trailhead: From exit 129 (Pinnacle) on US 52 north of Winston-Salem, take Perch Road west for 3.3 miles, then veer right onto Hauser Road. Follow Hauser Road for 2.2 miles; turn left again, still on Hauser Road, as the road you have been following becomes Caudle Road. Continue for 0.9 mile and turn left into the Yadkin River section of Pilot Mountain State Park. Trace the gravel road to make a pair of auto fords of Horne Creek. These fords are doable by your average SUV, except after heavy rains. If you feel uncomfortable with the auto ford, just walk the road. Either way, follow the road for 0.4 mile to the Horne Creek trailhead, which has a

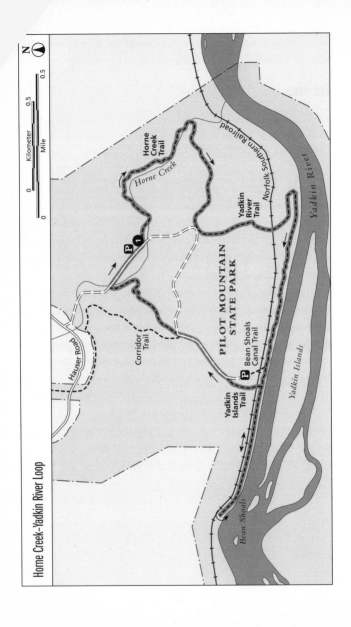

Horne Creek–Yadkin River Loop

picnic area and restrooms. This area is just before the third auto ford. GPS: N36 15.866' / W8 29.246'

The Hike

This trail explores the Yadkin River. It begins by tracing Horne Creek under a diverse forest of river birch, cedar, maple, beech, and holly. Green ferns soften the understory. Exposed tree roots help hold the soil in place along the stream as it spills over a bed of sand and rock. Occasional rock outcrops add to the scenery. Tributaries feed the creek, which gathers in pools divided by playful, sonorous shoals. After the trail turns away from Horne Creek, oaks dominate the forest as you rise to a low ridgeline before completing the Horne Creek Trail.

The hike then joins the Yadkin River Trail as it descends toward the Yadkin. Note the sunken nature of this old road and how a different track runs parallel to the left. In earlier days settlers often used a path until it became so eroded that they created a parallel trail. The trail reaches and crosses the active Norfolk Southern Railroad and then enters a wooded flat along the Yadkin. The Yadkin River begins in western North Carolina and flows east nearly to Winston-Salem before turning south, meeting the Uwharrie River to become the Pee Dee, which flows into South Carolina before exiting into the Atlantic near the city of Georgetown.

Along the trail the lowermost of the Yadkin River Islands appears and makes the river seem much narrower. Rocky Bean Shoals adds an audible dimension to the hike. Look for beaver slides heading into the river as well as trees that have been gnawed on or taken down by the animals. The path bypasses stone abutments of the railbed before it

dead–ends after reaching the westernmost of the Yadkin
River Islands. After backtracking, the hike leaves the river
and climbs over low hills before completing the loop.

Miles and Directions

0.0 Start the Horne Creek Trail near the third auto ford of Horne
Creek. Immediately cross a tributary on a footbridge. Travel
downstream along Horne Creek.

0.6 Rock-hop Horne Creek. Continue downstream along the
right-hand bank before turning away from the waterway altogether, rising on an old roadbed.

1.0 End the Horne Creek Trail and walk left on the gravel access
road for 50 yards. Turn left, joining the Yadkin River Trail as
it descends in lush woods.

1.5 Reach the Yadkin River. The trail curves sharply west, heading upstream.

2.1 The Bean Shoals Canal Trail leads right just a short distance
up to a parking area. Keep forward, still along the river.

2.2 The Yadkin Islands Trail heads right just before a short footbridge. This is your return route. Keep forward, still on the
Yadkin River Trail.

2.7 Yadkin River Trail dead-ends; backtrack.

3.2 Turn away from the river on the Yadkin Islands Trail. Immediately cross railroad tracks and keep descending on an old
roadbed.

3.4 Join the gravel access road and keep climbing.

3.6 Reach a hilltop. The gravel access road goes right; the Corri-
dor Trail heads left. Go straight on the white-blazed path into
shortleaf pines.

4.0 Reach Horne Creek on a gravel access road. Turn right;
immediately rock-hop Horne Creek and follow the access
road.

4.1 Arrive back at the trailhead.

2 Pilot Mountain Double Loop

This hike starts at the top of Pilot Mountain then leads past rock outcrops with fantastic views before dropping to the base of a cliff line where geological wonders await. You will see rock houses, sheer cliffs, and of course Ledge Spring. The views keep coming to the south. The second loop takes you around Big Pinnacle, where more cliffs impress and vistas extend to the Piedmont and beyond.

Distance: 2.6-mile double loop
Approximate hiking time: 2 to 2.5 hours
Difficulty: Moderate; rocky, slow trail in spots
Trail surface: Gravel, stone, leaves, sand
Best season: March through May; September through November
Other trail users: None
Canine compatibility: Leashed dogs permitted

Fees and permits: No fees or permits required
Schedule: Open 8:00 a.m. to sunset
Maps: USGS Pinnacle; Pilot Mountain State Park Hiking Trails; www.ncparks.gov/Visit/parks/pimo/pics/parkmap.pdf
Trail contact: Pilot Mountain State Park, 1792 Pilot Knob Park Rd., Pinnacle 27043; (336) 325-2355; www.ncparks.gov

Finding the trailhead: From the Pilot Mountain State Park exit on US 52 north of Winston-Salem, drive a short distance on the access road to reach the state park entrance. Continue on the main park road past the visitor center, heading toward the summit area. Follow it 2.2 miles to dead-end at the summit parking area. GPS: N36 20.447' / W80 28.782'

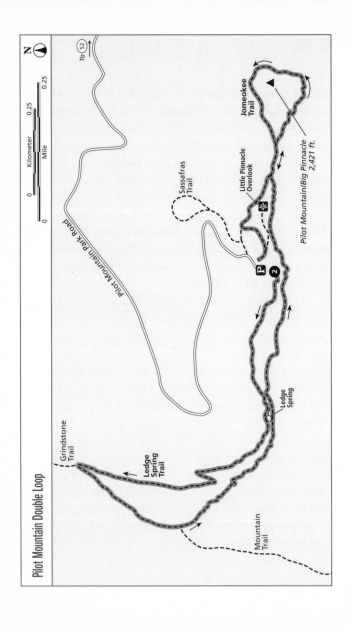

Pilot Mountain Double Loop

N

0   0.25
Kilometer
0   0.25
Mile

To 52

Pilot Mountain Park Road

Sassafras Trail

Grindstone Trail

Ledge Spring Trail

Mountain Trail

Ledge Spring

Jomeokee Trail

Little Pinnacle Overlook

Pilot Mountain/Big Pinnacle 2,421 ft.

P

2

The Hike

North Carolina has many special mountains, but as far as being a memorable landmark, Pilot Mountain—named for being a beacon to all who passed by—may be the most distinct. Located on the edge of the Piedmont, Pilot Mountain rises from the surrounding lands to climax in a circular peak of nearly vertical rock walls with a wooded cap. The park is now a great hiking destination, as well as a camping and climbing magnet for outdoors enthusiasts.

You'll be tempted to gaze out from the overlook at the parking lot, so go ahead and give it a gander before beginning your hike. This area can be busy with hikers and picnickers—and those who merely drive up here for the short walk to the overlook.

The first part of the hike takes you along the rim of a rock bluff that offers numerous southward views. The vistas are complemented by craggy pines and oaks growing amidst the gray rocks. Bronze pine needles sprinkling the forest floor add more color to the scenery. Occasional spur trails lead to outcrops overlooking the Piedmont to the south and east. The route drops from the bluff line then loops to the base of the cliff line upon which you were just hiking. The going is slow as you climb stone steps and work around massive boulders. Take your time and savor this area, watching for rock shelters, sheer bluffs, and water-worn crevices where plants have gained purchase. More views open to the south. You are hiking just below where you were earlier.

Pine-topped Pilot Mountain comes into view as the loop heads east. Sheer bluffs cast a rock cone, and evergreens at the top constitute a green crown.

Begin the second loop, which circles Pilot Mountain. This particular part of Pilot Mountain is also known as Big Pinnacle. Come alongside the multihued bluffs of Big Pinnacle, where water, elements, and time have left the stone walls gray and tan with tinges of black. These colorful geologic edifices rise higher than the earlier bluffs. In the eastern distance, the Sauratown Mountains appear, including the peaks at Hanging Rock State Park. Rhododendron thrives on the north side of the bluff as the trail circles around. On your return, don't pass up the short spur to the Little Pinnacle Overlook just before reaching the parking area.

Miles and Directions

0.0 Leave the vista point and trace the gravel track past a rock climbing registration area to join the yellow-blazed Ledge Spring Trail.

0.8 Stay left on the Ledge Spring Trail at a switchback as the Grindstone Trail heads right.

1.0 Stay on the Grindstone Trail as the Mountain Trail descends right. Continue alongside the base of a cliff line on a rocky, narrow path.

1.3 Ledge Springs emerges from the cliff line above and flows down a rock face.

1.8 Ledge Spring Trail meets the Jomeokee Trail. Continue on the Ledge Spring Trail and soon reach the second loop, which circles Pilot Mountain/Big Pinnacle. Look outward for distant views as well as upward at the impressive cliffs. Birds may be riding the hillside thermals.

2.2 Complete the second loop then stay right, heading toward the parking area.

2.5 Pass a spur trail leading left to Little Pinnacle.

2.6 Arrive back at the trailhead and parking area.

3 Hanging Rock

This busy out-and-back hike leads to a Triad landmark and lends its name to the state park it overlooks. From the park visitor center the hike climbs through woods to a rocky ridgeline, where pines and boulders form a scenic crest. From here daring hikers can walk out to the rock protrusion extending into the sky, where grand vistas open before them.

Distance: 2.4 miles out and back

Approximate hiking time: 1.5 to 2 hours

Difficulty: Moderate; 400-foot climb

Trail surface: Transitions from concrete to gravel to natural surface

Best season: March through May; September through November

Other trail users: None

Canine compatibility: Leashed dogs permitted

Fees and permits: No fees or permits required

Schedule: Open 8:00 a.m. to sunset

Maps: USGS Hanging Rock; Pilot Mountain State Park Hiking Trails; www.ncparks.gov/Visit/parks/haro/pics/parkmap.pdf

Trail contact: Hanging Rock State Park, 1792 Pilot Knob Park Rd., Pinnacle 27043; (336) 325-2355; www.ncparks.gov

Finding the trailhead: From Winston-Salem take US 52 north to exit 110B and turn left onto US 311. Follow US 311 north for 17 miles to NC 89. Go straight on NC 89 west for 9 miles to Hanging Rock Road. Turn left onto Hanging Rock Road and follow it for 1 mile to enter the state park. Follow the park road uphill to reach an intersection. Make a left turn toward the visitor center. The Hanging Rock Trail starts on the right-hand side as you enter the parking area. GPS: N36 23.661' / W80 15.980'

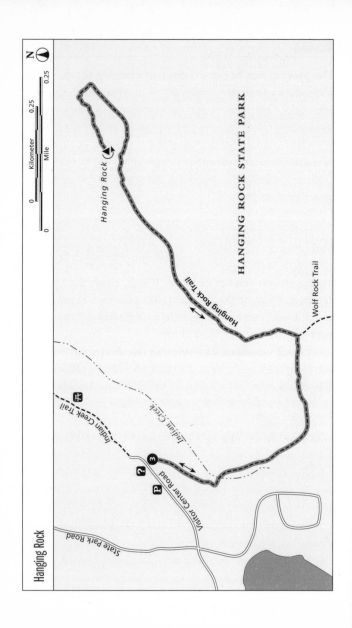

The Hike

The parking area has an overlook of Hanging Rock, a little ways down from the trailhead. You may want to view your goal. The trail to the promontory was once eroded and abused. But like most all the paths at Hanging Rock State Park, it has been reconstructed using a combination of materials and techniques designed to allow visitors to explore the landscape yet keep the resource preserved for future generations.

The trail to Hanging Rock is heavily used. As a result, the path was widely built with ample benches for relaxing. And upon seeing the view you will understand its popularity. Enjoy the first part of the trek while descending toward the uppermost reaches of Indian Creek, cloaked in rhododendron. Once at the stream, a 400-plus-foot climb stands ahead. Don't despair—the path is well graded and the ascent moderate for most of its distance.

A thick woodland of maple and oak shades the trail as it works up the highest ridge, from which Hanging Rock rises. The climb eases and allows you to catch your breath before the final scramble, which begins with stone and wood steps. The ridgeline narrows. More and more rock is exposed until you can see Hanging Rock protruding overhead. The path then circles around the south side of the knob, passing a holly-crowded cliff face before climbing step after stone step, leveling off in woodland of wind-pruned oaks, pines, and mountain laurel shading gray rocks and boulders.

The ridgeline narrows and the passage becomes constricted as you work toward Hanging Rock among the vegetation. Ahead the outcrop splits, with a deep chasm between two extensions. A USGS survey marker is on the right-hand promontory. It doesn't extend as far out as the left-hand promontory—a stone tongue reaching beyond a few scraggly pines hanging on for life.

Panoramic views open. Once out on the promontory, you will find spur trails leading to other outcrops where hikers explore for other views. The many boulders and rocks about make for excellent seating or picnicking spots. Give yourself time to hang out at Hanging Rock instead of rushing back to the trailhead.

Miles and Directions

0.0 Start on the Hanging Rock Trail as it leaves the farthest parking lot across from the visitor center. Descend on a wide stairway.

0.1 Cross Indian Creek, which flows through a culvert under the trail. This is the low point of the hike, which is mostly uphill from here.

0.2 The concrete trailbed gives way to gravel as it meanders up the uppermost hollow of Indian Creek.

0.5 Reach a gap and trail junction. The Hanging Rock Trail goes left and the Wolf Rock Trail leads right. Stay left, ascending toward Hanging Rock.

0.6 Reach the ridgeline of Hanging Rock. The walking is easy as you travel northeast through tall oaks.

0.9 The trail resumes climbing, working upwards on steps to the knob that is home to Hanging Rock.

1.1 Level out atop the knob of Hanging Rock. A rock outcrop near the trail offers views to the north.

1.2 Reach the stone tongue of Hanging Rock. Extensive views open. Spur trails lead to other outcrops. Stay awhile before retracing your steps.

2.4 Arrive back at the trailhead.

4 Moore's Wall Loop

This path makes a loop to reach an observation tower with 360-degree vistas atop one of Hanging Rock State Park's many geological features—Moore's Knob. After gently climbing along Cascade Creek, the trail toughens as it reaches the ridgeline of Moore's Wall and then cruises among boulders and cliff faces to attain Moore's Knob. The trail then passes Balanced Rock before dropping back to Cascade Creek and the trailhead.

Distance: 4.5-mile loop

Approximate hiking time: 2.5 to 3 hours

Difficulty: More challenging; an extended ascent

Trail surface: Forested trail with plenty of rock

Best season: March through May; September through November

Other trail users: None

Canine compatibility: Leashed dogs permitted

Fees and permits: No fees or permits required

Schedule: Open 8:00 a.m. to sunset

Maps: USGS Hanging Rock; Pilot Mountain State Park Hiking Trails; www.ncparks.gov/Visit/ parks/haro/pics/parkmap.pdf

Trail contact: Hanging Rock State Park, 1792 Pilot Knob Park Rd., Pinnacle 27043; (336) 325-2355; www.ncparks.gov

Finding the trailhead: From Winston-Salem take US 52 north to exit 110B and turn left onto US 311. Follow US 311 north for 17 miles to NC 89. Go straight on NC 89 west for 9 miles to Hanging Rock Road. Turn left onto Hanging Rock Road and follow it for 1 mile to enter the state park. Follow the road uphill to an intersection. The left turn goes to the visitor center; a right takes you to the campground. Continue straight toward the park lake, which offers swimming, boating, and picnicking. Continue for 0.3 mile to dead-end in a large parking area. The trail starts near the lake bathhouse. GPS: N36 23.440' / W80 16.012'

The Hike

The Civilian Conservation Corps (CCC) originally developed this state park, and their handiwork is visible as you pass the rock-and-wood bathhouse, impressive enough to be on the National Register of Historic Places. Moore's Wall rises beyond the serene park lake. A good eye will spot the squat observation tower that rises slightly above the tree line. That is your ultimate destination.

The first part of the hike squeezes up the uppermost Cascade Creek Valley, where evergreens crowd the hiker and trees provide thick shade. Narrow boardwalks cross streamlets and wetlands. Finally the trail leads to the drainage head and the forest transitions to oak. Beyond the intersection with the Tory's Den Trail, the white trailside blazes you see indicate the Mountains-to-Sea Trail (MST)—North Carolina's master path, which ranges from Clingmans Dome in the Smoky Mountains on the Tennessee state line to the Atlantic Ocean. The MST overlays the Moore's Wall Loop the rest of its distance.

The hike moderates once atop the ridge crest of Moore's Wall. Here pines and oaks stand contorted, twisted by the winds. Occasional vistas open from outcrops that beckon a stop. The best view waits at Moore's Knob, where a spur trail leads to an outcrop with a squat observation tower that affords 360-degree views. Pilot Mountain is visible to the west, the Blue Ridge to the northwest, and the Piedmont to the southeast. Note the pilings of a former tower and all the initials inscribed in the rock outcrop.

Continue along Moore's Wall as it curves northeasterly and loses elevation. The stone steps go a long way and you realize the amount of work done on a now-wider path. Soon pass the spur trail that leads left to Balanced Rock, on the northeast end of Moore's Wall. The descent continues to a feeder branch of Cascade Creek. A short climb follows until you pass through the park's fine campground. The final drop leads to Cascade Creek and the hike's end.

Miles and Directions

0.0 Start at the parking area and follow the wide service road toward the bathhouse. The trail starts on the left just before you reach the bathhouse.

0.1 Pass the trail to the picnic area and then the Chestnut Oak Nature Trail, which leads to Cooks Wall, rising from the south side of Cascade Creek.

0.3 Travel between rhododendrons and traverse a couple of boardwalks. Leave the lake to pass the second junction with the Chestnut Oak Nature Trail.

0.4 Reach the loop portion of the hike after crossing Cascade Creek on a short footbridge. Keep straight (clockwise), squeezing through mountain laurel, rhododendron, and thick woods on a slender path.

0.9 The Magnolia Springs Trail leads left toward Cooks Wall. Keep straight, climbing into rocky, oak-dominated woodland.

1.5 Level off in a gap to reach a junction with the Tory's Den Trail, which goes left. Remain on the Moore's Wall Loop Trail and begin climbing for the crest of Moore's Wall on a rocky track.

2.0 Reach the ridge crest and head easterly along Moore's Wall in thick woods.

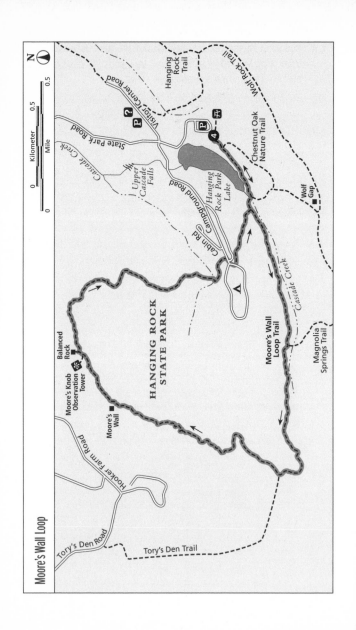

2.8 Reach an intersection with the spur trail to the observation tower atop Moore's Knob. The spur trail leads 50 yards to an outcrop and tower with panoramic views.

3.7 Continuing along Moore's Wall, the trail opens onto a rock slab and steps over a tributary of Cascade Creek.

3.9 Reach the campground access road. Turn right onto the road and stay left at the auto loop. Turn left into woods between Campsites 39 and 40. Keep descending.

4.1 Complete the loop portion of hike upon reaching junction at Cascade Creek; backtrack to the trailhead.

4.5 Arrive back at the trailhead.

5 Hidden and Window Falls

This hike leads to two of Hanging Rock State Park's four waterfalls. The ratio of rewards versus effort favors those who make this easy trek. You will first reach Hidden Falls, a cascade nestled in rhododendron. Next comes the showstopper— Window Falls. It is not just the falls in itself but the geological features surrounding it, including a literal window in a rock wall and a vista from a promontory above the falls.

Distance: 1.2 miles out and back
Approximate hiking time: 1 hour
Difficulty: Easy
Trail surface: Natural surfaces
Best season: November through May and after heavy rains
Other trail users: None
Canine compatibility: Leashed dogs permitted
Fees and permits: No fees or permits required

Schedule: Opens 8:00 a.m. to sunset
Maps: USGS Hanging Rock; Pilot Mountain State Park Hiking Trails; www.ncparks.gov/Visit/parks/haro/pics/parkmap.pdf
Trail contact: Hanging Rock State Park, 1792 Pilot Knob Park Rd., Pinnacle 27043; (336) 325-2355; www.ncparks.gov

Finding the trailhead: From Winston-Salem take US 52 north to exit 110B and turn left onto US 311. Follow US 311 north for 17 miles to NC 89. Go straight on NC 89 west for 9 miles to Hanging Rock Road. Turn left onto Hanging Rock Road and follow it for 1 mile to enter the state park. Follow the park road uphill to an intersection. Turn left, toward the visitor center. The Indian Creek Trail starts on the far end of the visitor center parking area. GPS: N36 23.731' / W80 15.900'

The Hike

Many other trails in Hanging Rock State Park start low and climb to a rock outcrop or other feature. In those cases you do your hard work on the front end. On this hike you actually start by going downhill to reach your destinations and then do your climbing—the hard work—on the way back. It can only be so hard, though, since this hike is only 0.6 mile each way; drops a little over 300 feet; and travels a top-notch, well-graded trail.

While you are here, make sure to stop at the lodgelike visitor center. The staffed facility offers interpretive information about the state park and may provide additional ideas concerning other park activities. Also, yet another waterfall can be bagged from the same parking area. Upper Cascades Falls can be reached via a 0.2-mile one-way all-access path that leaves the opposite end of the parking area from the Indian Creek Trail. A fourth waterfall, Lower Cascades Falls, is reached via a 0.4-mile one-way path off Hall Road.

The Indian Creek Trail is also part of the Mountains-to-Sea Trail, which traverses the park on its way from the Smoky Mountains to the Outer Banks. Chestnut oaks and pines shade the wide track as it passes several alluring picnic sites. Consider bringing lunch on this endeavor. Rustic large and small picnic shelters complete the outdoor dining options.

The trail narrows beyond the picnic shelters. The Indian Creek Trail, one of the park's newer paths, leads 3.6 miles to the Dan River. Wind downhill through oak-dominated woods with an understory of mountain laurel. After a few minutes of ridge walking, you might begin to wonder about your destination, as there is no water nearby. Then the trail drops into the Indian Creek Gorge and the sounds

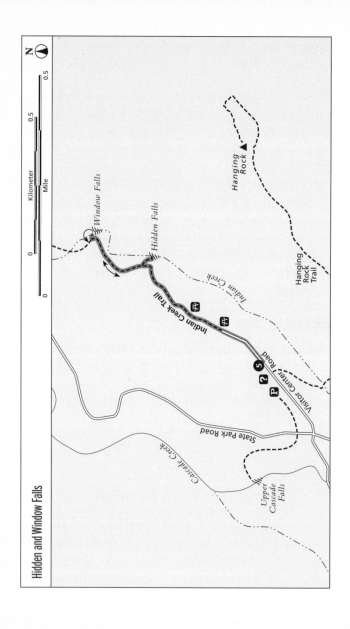

Hidden and Window Falls

of falling water reach your ears. You've arrived at your first destination—Hidden Falls. A spur trail leads to this cascade, which spills over a dark rock face framed in greenery.

The path becomes more primitive beyond Hidden Falls, rolling over a stone slab before reaching a massive rock protrusion. Here the main trail leads left, downhill, to a geological feature—an eroded window-size hole that opens astride Window Falls. The path continues down more steps to the base of Window Falls, where you can view the rock house below the falls, the 20-foot two-tiered cascade, and the stone promontory above the falls. A narrow sliding cascade tumbles for 30 or 40 feet down a chute below the falls.

Since the hike is short, allow yourself plenty of time to explore the falls and other geological features. The cliff above the falls offers a farther-reaching view.

Miles and Directions

0.0 Start on the Indian Creek Trail, leading from the northeast end of the visitor center parking area on a wide track that descends past picnic tables.

0.1 Pass the first of two historic stone-and-wood CCC-built picnic shelters.

0.4 Wide stone and wood steps lead to a junction. Here a spur trail leads right to Hidden Falls. Follow the trail 40 yards down to the 8-foot cascade as it spills over a stone lip and splashes off the rocks below.

0.6 Reach a rock cliff with views for those who follow it to its tip. The Indian Creek Trail leads left and circles below this promontory to an overlook of the rock window and Window Falls. More steps circle down to the base of falls. (FYI: This is an interesting geological area.) Retrace your path uphill to the trailhead.

1.2 Arrive back at the trailhead and visitor center parking area.

6 Bethabara Historic Hike

This trek back in time begins at the Bethabara Moravian village site, where you can gain some insight into how early area residents made their way in what was then a howling wilderness. A museum adds to the outdoor exhibits. Next, hike along streams that lead to a watery marsh, where an observation pier allows a view of a modern wilderness amid suburbia. Travel a marsh boardwalk that allows more aquatic integration before returning to the trailhead.

Distance: 2.3-mile loop
Approximate hiking time: 1.5 to 2 hours
Difficulty: Easy
Trail surface: Asphalt, natural surfaces, boardwalk
Best season: March through May; September through November
Other trail users: Bicyclists on greenway
Canine compatibility: Leashed dogs permitted on greenway
Fees and permits: No fees or permits required for trails or grounds; fee for museum
Schedule: Trails open year-round 8:00 a.m. to sunset; call for museum hours
Maps: USGS Rural Hall; Bethabara Trail; www.cityofws .org/Assets/CityOfWS/Docu ments/Recreation/Greenways/ bethabara_greenway_map.pdf
Trail contact: City of Winston-Salem Recreation & Parks Department, 2147 Bethabara Rd., Winston-Salem 27106; (336) 924-8191; www.cityofws.org/

Finding the trailhead: From Business I-40 in Winston-Salem, take exit 2B to Silas Creek Parkway (NC 67). Follow Silas Creek Parkway for 3 miles to a light. Stay left, still on Silas Creek Parkway, and continue for 2.2 miles to Bethabara Road. Turn left onto Bethabara Road and follow it for 0.5 mile to a parking area on the right, just before Bethabara Road becomes one lane. GPS: N36 09.291' / W80 17.798'

The Hike

This hike starts at Historic Bethabara Park, the preserved site of an early settlement. Back in 1753, German-speaking Moravians decided to call the land along Monarcas Creek home. Today you can see the restored 1788 church, Gemeinhaus, located adjacent to the trailhead. The grounds also include the ruins of other buildings and some reconstructed sites of small cabins and such displaying the life of the Moravians. I highly suggest touring the grounds before or after your hike and also checking out the museum.

Call ahead to make sure the museum is open. You can enjoy not only the re-created buildings but also the gardens and the re-created French and Indian War–era fort. Interpretive information gives you insight into the way of life of those who lived here two and a half centuries ago.

The hiking is easy—the trail is mostly level and partly paved. The natural setting is decidedly riparian, as you are constantly along tree-shaded streams and wetlands. Kids who love to play in the creek will rave about this hike.

Beyond Bethabara Village, the Bethabara Greenway meets and travels along Mill Creek, leaving the asphalt and joining a natural-surface trail that includes a stop at the Moravian mill site, which gave the name to Mill Creek.

Next comes the loop portion of the trek. The hike leads to a pier extending into a wetland and then joins a boardwalk adjacent to the swampy bog. Here nature is integrated into the city landscape. The wetland has many standing stumps, and a marsh boardwalk puts you directly in the mix. Your return route leads back along Mill Creek.

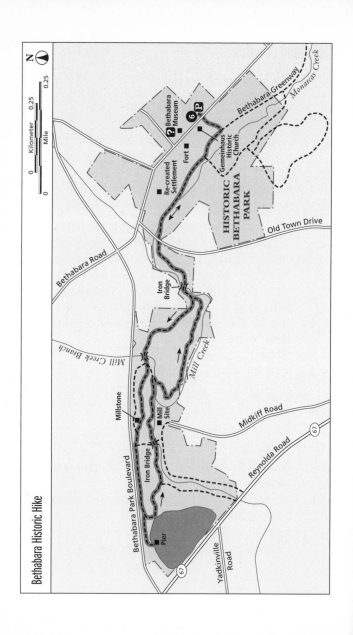

Bethabara Historic Hike

Miles and Directions

0.0 Start at the parking area on the east side of Bethabara Road. Cross the road and walk through the grass toward Monarcas Creek, keeping the Gemeinhaus Historic Church to your right.

0.1 Reach the asphalt Bethabara Greenway; turn right, heading northwest along Monarcas Creek.

0.2 A spur trail leads left across Monarcas Creek to God's Acre, the settlement cemetery. The re-created Bethabara settlement is to your right.

0.4 Cross Old Town Drive and angle left; rejoin the greenway, now along Mill Creek.

0.5 Cross an iron bridge over Mill Creek. The trail becomes a natural path. Your return route heads left just ahead. Stay right (counterclockwise) and begin the loop portion of the hike.

0.7 Cross Mill Creek Branch and reach an intersection. Keep straight on the wider main track as other trails head left and right.

0.9 Reach a millstone to the right of the trail. Pass two trail junctions and keep straight. Bethabara Park Boulevard is just to your right. You are now heading toward the marsh boardwalk and viewing pier.

1.1 The main loop heads left toward the Marsh Boardwalk. Keep right here and head toward the marsh wildlife-viewing pier. Backtrack and begin the marsh boardwalk, traveling approximately 150 yards on the boardwalk.

1.2 Reach Mill Creek and a trail junction. Stay left, keeping Mill Creek your right.

1.3 Reach an iron bridge crossing to an asphalt greenway that leads right to Reynolda Road and left to Midkiff Road. Keep straight along Mill Creek, passing the streamside foundation ruins of the 1755 Moravian mill.

1.5 Reach an intersection. Cross Mill Creek Branch right on a wooden bridge and then curve back toward larger Mill Creek.

1.8 Complete the loop portion of the hike after passing through Mill Creek bottoms. Bear right here and begin backtracking toward the Moravian settlement. If you haven't toured the grounds yet, do so, even if the museum isn't open.

2.3 Arrive back at the trailhead.

7 Salem Lake Loop

One of the Triad's earlier greenways, this hike makes an extended loop around Salem Lake. Leave the busy day-use area near the dam and then cruise the shoreline, winding into embayments and out to peninsulas. Watery views are plentiful along the mostly dirt track.

Distance: 6.9-mile loop

Approximate hiking time: 3 to 3.5 hours

Difficulty: More challenging due to distance

Trail surface: Asphalt, natural surfaces

Best season: March through May; September through November

Other trail users: Bicyclists

Canine compatibility: Leashed dogs permitted on greenway

Fees and permits: No fees or permits required

Schedule: Open winter 8:00 a.m. to 5:00 p.m.; spring, summer, and fall 7:00 a.m. to 8:00 p.m.

Maps: USGS Winston-Salem East; Salem Creek and Lake Trail; www.cityofws.org/Assets/City OfWS/Documents/Recreation/ Greenways/salem_lake_creek_ greenway_map.pdf

Trail contact: City of Winston-Salem Recreation & Parks Department, 1001 Salem Lake Rd., Winston-Salem 27106; (336) 727-2063; www.cityofws .org/

Finding the trailhead: From Business I-40 in Winston-Salem, take exit 6C (Martin Luther King Jr. Drive). Follow Martin Luther King Jr. Drive south for 0.8 mile, passing through Winston-Salem State University, to reach Reynolds Park Road. Turn left onto Reynolds Park Road and follow it for 1.9 miles to Salem Lake Road. Turn left onto Salem Lake Road and follow it for 0.6 mile to dead-end at Salem Lake Park. Park near the pier. GPS: N36 5.732 / W80 11.561

The Hike

If you are looking to break into a longer hike, this is a good one to start with. Despite a paved beginning, the vast majority of the trail is gravel or natural surfaces, which are easier on the feet. Elevation changes are minimal, which makes the distance more doable.

Tall pines and hardwoods shade the wide trail, which is popular with joggers and bicyclists as well is hikers. Resting benches are placed sporadically along the trail. Occasional singletrack paths, created by mountain bikers, spur off the main trail. Oak, beech, dogwood, and elm are just a few of the trees that will shade you. Sweet gum and cedar line the way as well. Note the occasional rocky areas along the trail and shoreline. A practiced eye will spot old roadbeds and even homesites along the way. In spring, jonquils and other plantings bloom at these former homes.

You may want to consider bringing lunch, and most definitely bring water—this is a long trek.

The hike starts off with a surprise as you circle behind the lake dam and hear the spillway splashing into Salem Creek. Here the Salem Creek Greenway journeys to Old Salem and downtown Winston-Salem.

Since the Salem Lake Trail stays along the shoreline virtually its entire distance, hikers are rewarded with ever-changing vantages of the 365-acre impoundment. There are occasional vistas of the pier and the main day-use area. On most hikes you can't see your beginning and end point. You can on this one, which makes these vistas more interesting.

There is a second access off Linville Road, but the parking area is very small and will almost certainly be full on weekends and nice afternoons. There is ample parking at the main day-use area, including a large gravel trailhead parking area that is open year-round except January and February.

Miles and Directions

0.0 Start at the parking area. Looking out on the pier, head left through a metal fence gate and then join an asphalt path heading downhill toward the base of the lake dam. Cross a low-water bridge over Salem Creek to reach a junction. Here the Salem Creek Greenway heads left to downtown. Stay right, heading uphill to come alongside Salem Lake.

0.5 Reach a trail junction. Here a dirt track leads left up the Lowery Creek arm of Salem Lake. This hike veers right to cross the Lowery Creek embayment on a bridge.

0.8 Begin circling into a second embayment.

1.4 A clear vista opens to the west of the pier and day-use area. Begin heading up the long Kerners Mill Creek embayment, winding in and out of hollows cut by intermittent stream-beds.

2.3 Pass through a dense pine grove.

2.6 Walk under a power line.

3.0 Reach Linville Road Southeast. Turn right, following a paved track to reach the Linville Road parking area. Turn right again, resuming a dirt track and begin your return journey.

3.4 Walk under the power line a second time.

3.6 Pass a large inscribed beech tree to the left of the trail, then circle around a large embayment.

3.7 Cross the embayment on a land bridge. A wetland pond stands to your left.

4.4 Reach a noteworthy vista looking southwest at the main day-use area. Curve into a smaller embayment.

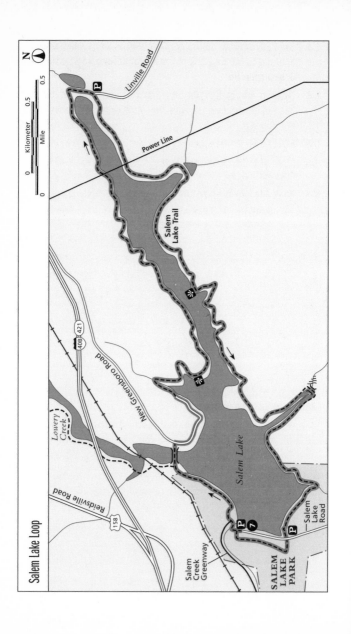

Salem Lake Loop

5.1 The trail briefly leaves Salem Lake and ascends a hill before returning to the water. Winter views of downtown Winston-Salem open up.

5.6 Cross an iron bridge over an unnamed rocky stream at the head of an embayment. Note the small waterfalls upstream of the bridge.

6.5 Reach a large gravel parking area and cross Salem Lake Road. (FYI: This parking area is closed in January and February.) Ascend, now on asphalt. Make a hard right atop a hill.

6.9 Arrive back at the trailhead, completing the loop.

8 Bald Eagle Loop

This hike travels the banks and wetlands of Brush Creek on its way to Lake Higgins, one of Greensboro's municipal watershed lakes. As you near Lake Higgins, the hike loops up a densely wooded valley feeding Brush Creek. Finally the loop leads to the shores of the Lake Higgins, where views await before you backtrack to the trailhead. Hikers have the additional option of returning via the Beech Bluff Trail.

Distance: 3.3-mile lollipop
Approximate hiking time: 1.5 to 2 hours
Difficulty: Moderate
Trail surface: Natural surfaces
Best season: March through May; September through November
Other trail users: Mountain bikers, joggers
Canine compatibility: Leashed dogs permitted
Fees and permits: No fees or permits required

Schedule: Open sunrise to sunset year-round
Maps: USGS Summerfield; Eagle Trail; www.greensboro-nc.gov/ NR/rdonlyres/A8865778-D4F5- 48C0-BE0F-BF648FE3169A/0/ WatershedHigginsSection.pdf
Trail contact: Greensboro Parks & Recreation Department, 1001 Fourth St., Greensboro 27405; (336) 373-2574; www .greensboro-nc.gov/ departments/Parks

Finding the trailhead: From exit 212B on I-40 west of downtown Greensboro, take I-840 east for 2.8 miles to exit 3 (Bryan Boulevard/PTI Airport). Follow Bryan Boulevard east to the Fleming Road exit. Follow Fleming Road north for 2.6 miles to Brass Eagle Loop. Turn right onto Brass Eagle Loop and follow it 0.2 mile to Long Valley Road. Turn right onto Long Valley Road and follow it a short distance to the trailhead on your right. GPS: N36 08.493' / W79 54.740'

The Hike

The trailhead parking area is small. If it is full, you can park on the other side of the Brush Creek at the Beech Bluff trailhead.

The Bald Eagle Trail, marked with metal white-diamond blazes, is popular with mountain bikers. Keep your eyes and ears peeled as you walk the singletrack path in rich, vine-draped woods with the brush of Brush Creek to your right. The path straddles the margin where dry land meets marsh, allowing you to enjoy the varied ecosystems. Pines, sweet gum, and oaks rise overhead. Their roots form obstacles across the trailbed that will catch the toe of the unwary walker.

The loop portion of the hike leaves Brush Creek and wanders through thickly wooded hills, exploring a portion of the watershed property that's mostly well away from water. The loop trail is much less used than the main path and thus offers a narrower tread and more solitude. Tree cover is also denser, with pines growing ultrathick in places. This mini-wilderness provides a habitat for wildlife—you may see a deer or two as you're hiking.

Ramble through hills to top out, traveling nowhere in particular, just making the most of the available terrain before descending toward Lake Higgins and intersecting the Bald Eagle Trail. Turn right onto Bald Eagle Trail and enjoy views of Lake Higgins before completing the loop and backtracking to the trailhead.

Option: Rather than backtracking to Long Valley Road you could walk left to Lewiston Road, cross the lake on Lewiston Road, turn right, and join the Beech Bluff Trail. This 1.3-mile hiker-only path travels a northwest-facing hill-

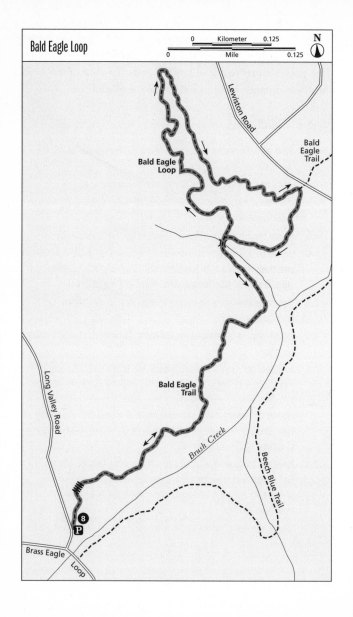

Bald Eagle Loop

Bald Eagle Loop

Bald Eagle Trail

Bald Eagle Trail

Lewiston Road

Long Valley Road

Brass Eagle Loop

Brush Creek

Beech Blue Trail

8
P

Kilometer
0   0.125
Mile
0   0.125

N

side, which is a cooler and moister site favoring its namesake beech trees. It is also a good spring wildflower destination. The path returns to Brass Eagle Loop. You can then walk the short distance to the Long Valley trailhead.

Miles and Directions

0.0 Start at the parking area and take the singletrack trail leading northeast into the thick woods.

0.1 Dip into a wetland spanned by a boardwalk.

0.5 Pass through a clearing after nearing houses. Pass through a second clearing.

0.6 Leave the houses and enter a larger tract of woodland.

1.0 Dip to bridge a stream. Traverse a wetland on a boardwalk and then reach a trail junction. the Bald Eagle Trail leads right. Bear left (clockwise) onto the Bald Eagle Loop.

1.1 Return to the creek you just crossed and begin heading upstream along it.

1.6 Reach your most northwesterly point, then curve toward Lake Higgins.

2.1 Intersect the Bald Eagle Trail after passing over a couple of small plank bridges. Lewiston Road is within sight to your left. The Bald Eagle Trail continues across Lewiston Road to end at a parking area off Hamburg Mill Road, 3.0 miles distant. Turn right here, away from Lewiston Road. Views open of Lake Higgins to your left.

2.3 Reach a trail junction. You have been here before. The Bald Eagle Loop leads right; bear left and then keep straight, crossing a boardwalk and bridging a stream, now backtracking.

3.3 Reach the Long Valley Road trailhead, completing the hike.

9 Bur-Mil Park: Big Loop

A perfect leg stretcher or daily training hike, this trek makes a woodland loop through the western part of Bur-Mil Park, a former recreation area for Burlington Mills employees. The hike traces a stream toward Lake Brandt, following the lake contours before turning away from the impoundment and heading up a different streambed to high ground.

Distance: 2.0-mile loop

Approximate hiking time: 1 to 1.5 hours

Difficulty: Easy

Trail surface: Natural surfaces

Best season: March through May; September through November

Other trail users: Bicyclists

Canine compatibility: Leashed dogs permitted

Fees and permits: No fees or permits required

Schedule: Open year-round 8:00 a.m. to sunset

Maps: USGS Lake Brandt and Summerfield; Bur-Mil Park Trails; www.greensboro-nc.gov/NR/rdonlyres/31A4D17D-8192-4D9A-A930-714D72B60A6E/0/ParksBurMil.pdf

Trail contact: Bur-Mil Park, 5834 Bur-Mil Club Rd., Greensboro 27410; (336) 373-3800; www.greensboro-nc.gov/departments/Parks/

Finding the trailhead: From Bryan Boulevard, northwest of downtown Greensboro, take Westridge Road east for 1 mile to Battleground Road. Turn left onto Battleground Road (US 220 North) and follow it for 3.3 miles to Owls Roost Road. Turn right onto Owls Roost Road and follow it 0.3 mile to Bur-Mil Club Road. Turn left onto Bur-Mil Club Road to enter Bur-Mil Park and take the first left to park at the aquatic center. The trail starts near the north end of the parking area, briefly following a concrete path toward a playground. GPS: N36 09.756' / W79 52.253'

The Hike

Bur-Mil Park is a multiple-use facility run by the city of Greensboro but owned by Guilford County. The Big Loop Trail is the longest path entirely within Bur Mil Park and connects to the Lake Brandt Greenway. The Big Loop Trail offers an undulating walk in the hills, through streamside and lakeside environments, and makes for an ideal easy day hike that is long enough to give daily exercise value yet not be overly strenuous. The natural trail surface is easy on the feet and knees, as opposed to concrete or asphalt trails. While hiking, keep an ear peeled for mountain bikers, who also like to utilize the path.

The relaxing setting in the midst of suburban Greensboro starts at the loop portion of the hike. Contemplation benches are stationed here for those who want to slow down life's hectic pace before or after their hike. Your clockwise loop travels beneath a forest of beech, cedar, and sweet gum in addition to oak.

The park is laced with water features, and you soon pass over an intermittent streambed, nearing Owls Roost Road. The path then heads north, roughly paralleling a watercourse that flows toward Lake Brandt. The rocky streambeds are softened by ferns lining their courses. Battleground Road lies uphill to the left. Lake Brandt comes into sight after the trail curves easterly. Watch for club moss, actually a member of the fern family, rising from the forest floor. Spongy and bright green, it almost looks fake. Pines also increase in number among the hills above the lake.

The forest changes yet again as the Big Loop Trail turns south. Here a moist north-facing hollow shelters gray-trunked tulip trees standing sentinel along the path. As you

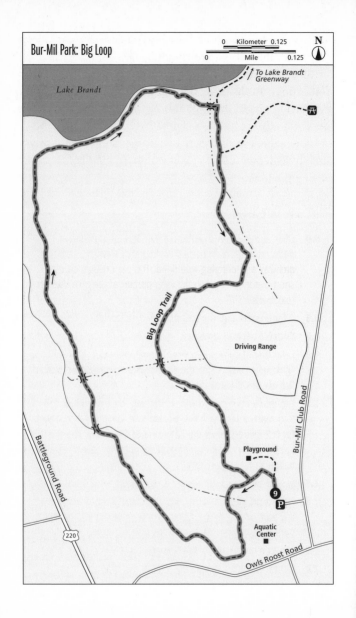

Bur-Mil Park: Big Loop

0   Kilometer 0.125

0   Mile   0.125

N

Lake Brandt

To Lake Brandt
Greenway

Big Loop Trail

Driving Range

Bur-Mil Club Road

Playground

9

P

Battleground Road

220

Aquatic
Center

Owls Roost Road

head up the hollow, note how heavy rains have cut a deep gorge into the hills you're climbing.

Since this park is a multi-use facility, trails pass near other destinations. In this case, the Big Loop Trail circles around the driving range. Bur-Mil also has a par-3 golf course for those who like to swing a club. Watch out for golf balls!

For hikers the final part of the Big Loop Trail weaves among fields and woods, passing a playground before completing the loop.

Miles and Directions

0.0 Start at the aquatic center parking area on a concrete path. Look left for a natural-surface trail traveling under an archway and entering woodland. The path descends but a short distance to reach the loop portion of the hike. Bear left (clockwise).

0.5 After descending, the trail bridges a streamlet.

0.6 Bridge a second streamlet.

0.9 Lake Brandt comes into view through the trees. The Big Loop Trail curves easterly to roughly parallel the lakeshore, which lies about 65 yards distant.

1.2 Dip into a ravine filled with tulip trees; bridge a streamlet and reach a trail junction. Here a lakeside trail goes straight for 0.2 mile to reach the Lake Brandt Greenway. The Big Loop Trail turns right on a narrower path and heads up the ravine along a streamlet.

1.3 A spur trail leads left up to Picnic Shelter #4. Stay straight.

1.4 Pass a tall stand of exotic bamboo sheltering a house near the park driving range. Once atop the hill, the trail makes a hard right and circles around the driving range.

1.6 Dip to a ravine and cross a wooden bridge.

2.0 Return to trailhead after completing the loop.

10 Bur-Mil Park: Little Loop

This hike combines the popular Lake Brandt Greenway with the seldom-traveled Little Loop Trail, which explores rolling woodland in the southeast corner of Bur-Mil Park. Since you start at Bur-Mil Park Wildlife Education Center, consider combining this trek with a visit to the center. If you want to extend your hike, the Lake Brandt Greenway travels in both directions beyond the Little Loop Trail.

Distance: 1.2-mile lollipop

Approximate hiking time: 1 hour

Difficulty: Easy

Trail surface: Asphalt greenway and forested trail

Best season: March through May; September through November

Other trail users: Bicyclists

Canine compatibility: Leashed dogs permitted

Fees and permits: No fees or permits required

Schedule: Open year-round 8:00 a.m. to sunset

Maps: USGS Lake Brandt; Bur-Mil Park Trails; www .greensboro-nc.gov/NR/ rdonlyres/31A4D17D-8192-4D9A-A930-714D72B60A6E/0/ ParksBurMil.pdf

Trail contact: Bur-Mil Park, 5834 Bur-Mil Club Rd. Greensboro 27410; (336) 373-3800; www.greensboro-nc.gov/ departments/Parks/

Finding the trailhead: From Bryan Boulevard, northwest of downtown Greensboro, take Westridge Road east for 1 mile to Battleground Road (US 220 North). Turn left onto Battleground Road and follow it for 3.3 miles to Owls Roost Road. Turn right onto Owls Roost Road and follow it 0.3 mile to Bur-Mil Club Road. Turn left onto Bur-Mil Club Road to enter Bur-Mil Park and stay straight for 0.7 mile to dead-end at the wildlife education center. The trail starts behind the center. GPS: N36 10.150' / W79 52.037'

The Hike

The Bur-Mil Park wildlife education center, named for Frank Sharpe Jr., is situated in a renovated barn that has been on the property since the early 1900s. You can enjoy the nature programs and displays at no charge. Classes at the center include Wildlife for Every Season, All about Insects, nature photography, and even beginner fly fishing. For anglers who want to enjoy the pond this hike travels by, the wildlife education center sells bait and licenses and will even loan you a rod. Consider timing your hike with a class offered at the center. Class schedules are available on the Greensboro parks Web site.

The first part of this hike travels the Lake Brandt Greenway. The greenway is a bona fide "rail trail," meaning it actually travels over an abandoned railroad bed for most of its distance. It is an artery path that connects to many trails in the greater Greensboro system, including several of the watershed trails and the trails at Guilford Courthouse National Military Park, which are included in the guidebook.

Ironically, the first part of the greenway you travel is actually a reroute off the railbed. The old railroad grade was flooded beneath the waters of the fishing lake along which the trail travels. You may see waterfowl in the lake as you stroll along. Anglers will be vying for bass, bream, and catfish as they watch their poles for the slightest tug.

Solitude will be yours upon leaving the greenway and joining the narrow and primitive Little Loop Trail. A dense forest of pine, oak, beech, and maple crowds the path and provides deep summer shade. The path twists and turns, going where you think it might not or shouldn't go, nearly returning to the fishing lake.

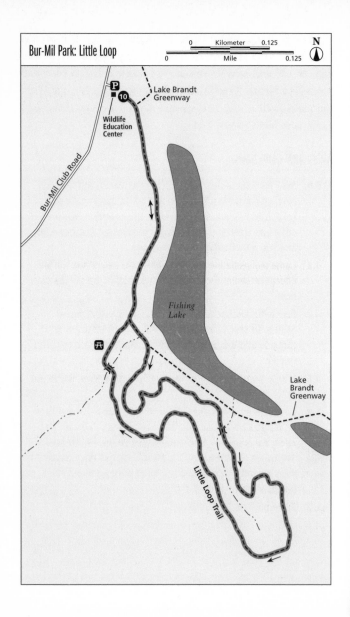

Bur-Mil Park: Little Loop

0   Kilometer   0.125
0   Mile   0.125

N

Lake Brandt
Greenway

Wildlife
Education
Center

Bur-Mil Club Road

Fishing
Lake

Lake
Brandt
Greenway

Little Loop Trail

Travel along a bluff that overlooks the greenway and lake. Part of the trail travels near private property. Here you can see old and new Carolina—a historic tobacco barn and a modern house. The Triad is changing and growing. Having parks such as this keeps some natural aspects of the area easily accessible to residents.

Miles and Directions

0.0   Start behind the education center and join an asphalt path, heading downhill. Walk just a short distance and join the Lake Brandt Greenway. To your left the greenway heads north and crosses Lake Brandt. You, however, keep straight, heading southbound on the greenway.

0.1   Come alongside the slender fishing lake behind the wildlife education center. Walkers and anglers alike use the benches here.

0.2   Reach the loop portion of your hike. To the right, Picnic Shelter #8 stands in a small clearing. Bear left just a short distance and the singletrack Little Loop Trail heads right into woods.

0.5   Bridge a small stream emanating from the hollow, which you circle around.

1.0   Complete the Little Loop Trail, emerging into a clearing near Picnic Shelter #8 just after bridging a stream. Veer left and rejoin the greenway, backtracking toward the wildlife education center. (**Option:** For good views consider going beyond the trailhead on the greenway, which opens onto a trail bridge spanning Lake Brandt.)

1.2   Arrive back at the trailhead.

11 Guilford Courthouse Loop

This loop hike explores Greensboro's preserved Revolutionary War battlefield—Guilford Courthouse National Military Park. After learning about this important engagement at the visitor center, you can take the hiker–only path past informative displays, monuments, and other interpretive information amid a scenic setting.

Distance: 2.1-mile loop
Approximate hiking time: 1.5 to 2 hours
Difficulty: Easy
Trail surface: Rock-encrusted asphalt
Best season: March through May; September through November
Other trail users: None
Canine compatibility: Leashed dogs permitted

Fees and permits: No fees or permits required
Schedule: Open year-round 8:30 a.m. to 5 p.m.
Maps: USGS map: Lake Brandt; Guilford Courthouse National Military Park; www.nps.gov/guco/
Trail contact: Guilford Courthouse National Military Park, 2332 New Garden Rd., Greensboro 27410; (336) 288-1776; www.nps.gov/guco

Finding the trailhead: From downtown Greensboro take Battleground Road (US 220 North) for 7 miles to New Garden Road. Turn right onto New Garden Road and follow it for 0.3 mile to turn into the park entrance road. Park near the visitor center, where the hike starts. GPS: N36 7.906' / W79 50.766'

The Hike

This is an opportunity to combine a hike with a walking tour of a historic Revolutionary War battlefield. The leader of the American side, Nathanael Greene, is the man for whom Greensboro is named. First stop at the visitor center and at least view the ten-minute tactical film explaining the battle. The thirty-minute film is even better. Other displays have artifacts form the actual engagement.

The hiker-only trail roughly parallels the auto tour route, stopping at seven of the eight official tour stops. Oaks and pines dominate the woodlands here, which are interspersed with clearings. You will see numerous monuments and also travel part of historic New Garden Road, the reason the battle occurred here in the first place.

At the time of the 1781 battle, the area was a mix of fields and woods. The Americans hung back in the woods, firing at the British as they crossed open fields. You will twice cross Richland Creek, which also played a large role in the battle, as the line of veteran American soldiers positioned themselves on an eastern rise above the creek. While traveling the landscape, now in the middle of Greensboro, imagine soldiers on both sides attempting to use the terrain to their advantage.

The monuments also tell part of the story, honoring heroes who died that day and others who lived to tell the story. Interestingly, the battlefield was first preserved by a private group, the Guilford Battle Ground Company, in 1887. Led by David Schenck, the group was appalled at the sorry condition of the battlefield and took it upon themselves to preserve the site, mark battlefield locations, and erect monuments of their own. Modern historians, using today's technology, improved on the private group's work. The site, now managed by the National Park Service, maintains an important slice of North Carolina's past.

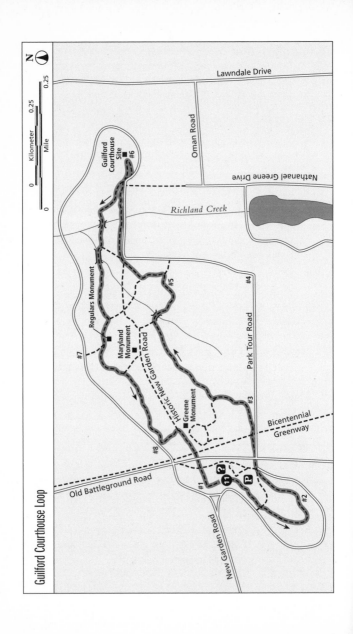

Guilford Courthouse Loop

Miles and Directions

0.0 Start at the visitor center entrance and go right a short distance to Tour Stop #1, Monument Row. Return to the visitor center and cross the parking area to begin the asphalt hiker-only trail.

0.2 Pass Tour Stop #2, site of the American First Line, where ragtag North Carolina militia fired muskets at the advancing British troops.

0.4 Use care as you cross Old Battleground Road. The Bicentennial Greenway heads north and south. The hike continues straight, passing Tour Stop #3 before heading left into deep woods. The American Second Line, Virginia militia, was stationed here along a northward axis.

0.6 Reach a T junction. Keep right here. The trail going left heads toward Tour Stop #8 and the Greene Monument.

0.8 Reach a junction. The left-hand trail leads to Historic New Garden Road. Keep right, spanning a creek on a bridge then climbing toward Tour Stop #5. Keep north to the next junction and then bear right, heading toward Tour Stop #6. Soon join Historic New Garden Road and head east, coming directly alongside Park Tour Road.

1.2 Reach the American Third Line Trail, which heads left toward cannons stationed in the woods. A paved trail heads right toward Country Park. Continue straight toward Tour Stop #6. Check out the Guilford Courthouse site before returning to the Third Line Trail.

1.4 Bridge Richland Creek after passing American cannon on the Third Line Trail. Stay right at the following junction, immediately bridging a tributary of Richland Creek and climbing.

1.6 Reach an intersection; stay right, heading toward Tour Stop #7. Soon pass the Regulars Monument and Tour Stop #7. A spur trail leads right to Park Tour Road.

1.7 Reach a junction. Stay straight as a leftward trail leads to the Maryland Monument.

1.9 Reach Tour Stop #8, a monument to David Schenck. Head left toward the Greene Monument to shortly reach Historic New Garden Road. Turn right onto the road.

2.0 Cross Bicentennial Greenway and then Old Battleground Road.

2.1 Reach the visitor center after passing Tour Stop #1, completing the loop.

12 Laurel Bluff Out-and-Back

The Laurel Bluff Trail is widely regarded as one of Greens-boro's most scenic watershed trails. It certainly offers varied habitats. The hiker–only path travels along Reedy Fork, exploring lush bottoms and steep hillsides where mountain laurel and beech trees thrive. It then saddles alongside a froggy marsh before ascending a hill overlooking Lake Townsend, where a view awaits. Look for more beauty on your return trip.

Distance: 3.6 miles out and back
Approximate hiking time: 2 to 2.5 hours
Difficulty: Moderate; some steep sections
Trail surface: Natural surfaces
Best season: March through May; September through November
Other trail users: Joggers
Canine compatibility: Leashed dogs permitted
Fees and permits: No fees or permits required

Schedule: Open sunrise to sunset
Maps: USGS Lake Brandt; Greensboro Watershed Trails; www.greensboro-nc.gov/NR/ rdonlyres/7F22D167-53C3-42F0-8D72-881148C884F2/0/ WatershedReedySection.pdf
Trail contact: Greensboro Parks & Recreation Department, 1001 Fourth St., Greensboro 27405; (336) 373-2574; www .greensboro-nc.gov/ departments/Parks

Finding the trailhead: From downtown Greensboro take Battle-ground Road (US 220 North) for 6 miles to Old Battleground Road. Turn right onto Old Battleground Road and follow it for 1.5 miles to Lake Brandt Road. Turn right onto Lake Brandt Road. Travel for 1.2 miles to a traffic light and turn left, still on Lake Brandt Road. Drive for a total of 2.5 miles on Lake Brandt Road to a parking area on your right, before crossing Reedy Fork below Lake Brandt Dam. The parking area is next to the Greensboro Lake Brandt Waterworks Station. GPS: N36 10.180' / W79 50.204'

The Hike

This one-way trail is maintained by the local Audubon Society. It wanders along Reedy Fork and the upper margins of Lake Townsend between Lake Brandt Road and North Church Street. The trail in its entirety is 3.5 miles—a 7.0-mile round-trip—perhaps more than you bargained for.

This segment of the trail travels along Reedy Fork, with its extensive, sometimes-flooded bottoms, then beside a transitional marsh area. Finally the marsh gives way to the open waters of Lake Townsend, a long reservoir with trails lacing its north and south shorelines. In fact, a hiker can walk Lake Townsend's south shore all the way from Lake Brandt Road to Bryan Park—a distance of 11.5 trail miles—with just a little road walk on North Church Street.

Those troubled by mountain bike traffic on some of the other Greensboro watershed trails will enjoy the hiker-only status of this track. Since this path travels along the north-facing slope of Reedy Fork, it is a good spring wildflower destination. After some initial twisting and turning amid Greensboro's infrastructure, the Laurel Bluff Trail travels alongside a steep, wooded bluff in a purely natural setting.

The track then ascends the bluff, rolling amid hardwoods dispersed enough to allow views of Reedy Fork below. The drainage pattern of the stream becomes evident from this elevated locale. The main channel flows unimpeded, yet you can see other sloughs and channels that flow at higher water levels to become ponds or dry out altogether when stream flow decreases.

Next the path mixes in some bottomland exploration where creek meets lake to create an amphibian-rich marsh before making a final climb to a cleared bluff well above Lake Townsend. This is where you find unimpeded views of the lake and the surrounding hills. Though the clearing works as a rewarding destination, it was not created for altruistic reasons—a small landing strip is located in a flat above the lake. This is your turnaround point. Should you choose to walk the entire Laurel Bluff Trail, it is 1.7 miles farther to North Church Street.

Miles and Directions

0.0 Standing with Lake Brandt Road to your back and the Greensboro Lake Brandt Waterworks Station to your left, walk away from the road along a metal fence bordering the waterworks station. Look for the hiker trail sign and curve along the fence line, shortly leaving the waterworks station and heading downhill to reach a large stand of bamboo.

0.2 Bridge a small stream after winding through a wide bottom. Shortly bisect a power line clearing.

0.3 Pass through a gas line clearing.

0.5 Reach Reedy Fork. The trail then leaves bottomland and ascends a bluff dominated by beech trees. The now-elevated path offers a commanding view of the Reedy Fork bottomlands.

0.6 Drop off the bluff to step over a pair of tributaries. Quickly resume the hillside on a steep bluff, passing the mountain laurel for which the trail is named.

1.1 Leave the bluff and walk through a level, wooded bottomland.

1.2 Cross a boardwalk and then bridge a feeder branch as you near the marsh of Lake Townsend.

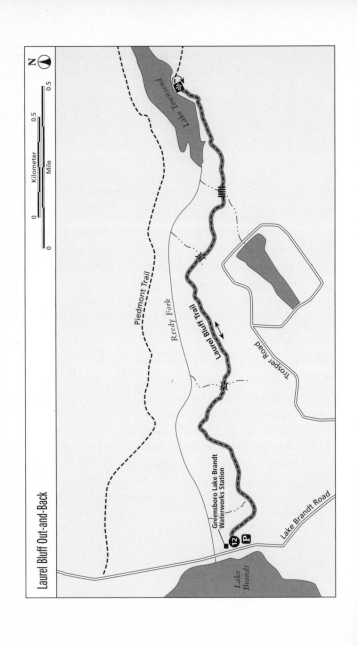

Laurel Bluff Out-and-Back

1.3 Lake Townsend comes into view through the trees after the trail crosses one more streambed. Climb a wooded hill above the water.

1.8 Reach a clearing atop a steep bluff with a clear vista of Lake Townsend. This is your turnaround point. Backtrack at your leisure.

3.6 Arrive back at the trailhead.

13 Northeast Park Loop

This loop hike travels through part of the extensive trail system of one of Guilford County's newest parks. The trek will lead you past overlooks of Reedy Fork and also along its tributary—Buffalo Creek. The trail then winds through a young forest in flatwoods before emerging at a picnic shelter. Cut through the heart of the park and its developed facilities to complete the loop.

Distance: 2.3-mile loop
Approximate hiking time: 1 to 2 hours
Difficulty: Easy; a few hills
Trail surface: Natural surfaces, a little asphalt
Best season: March through May; September through November
Other trail users: Mountain bikers on parts of loop
Canine compatibility: Leashed dogs permitted

Fees and permits: No fees or permits required
Schedule: Open 8:00 a.m. to 8:00 p.m. spring, summer, fall; 8:00 a.m. to 6:00 p.m. winter
Maps: USGS Ossipee; Northeast Park Trail System; www.northeastpark.info/Trails.html
Trail contact: Northeast Park, 3421 Northeast Park Dr., Gibsonville 27249; (336) 375-7722; www.northeastpark.info

Finding the trailhead: From exit 138 on I-40/I-85 between Greensboro and Burlington, take NC 61 north for 7.9 miles, passing through Gibsonville along the way, to reach Huffine Mill Road. Turn left onto Huffine Mill Road and follow it for 2.9 miles to High Rock Road. Turn right onto High Rock Road and follow it 0.1 mile, then turn right into Northeast Park. Follow the main park road to a traffic circle and then veer left. Follow this road for 0.3 mile to reach a picnic shelter and restrooms on your left. The trail access is between picnic shelter and restrooms. GPS: N36 10.165' / W79 36.428'

The Hike

Northeast Park was developed with trails in mind, rather than just integrating trails into an already existing park. More than just pathways, the park is a multiuse destination attracting visitors from fast-growing Northeast Guilford County and beyond. The park also has equestrian facilities, ball fields, picnic shelters, mountain biking trails, a swimming pool, and even a canoe launch for those wishing to enjoy nature via water.

This particular hike explores the eastern side of the park. It begins traversing bluffs well above Reedy Fork, a canoeable stream. Enjoy a couple of developed overlooks before descending to the stream bottom on the Bear Hollow Trail. Here you bisect the Low Water Crossing trailhead to join the Buffalo Creek Trail as it curves along alluring Buffalo Creek, with its alternating pools and shoals. Fallen logs and sandbars add to the scenery. Take note of the rock outcrops along the watercourse and on the streambanks and trail.

The scenery changes once you leave the streams. The hike travels through low evergreens, sometimes in the open sun, winding where you think it won't or shouldn't go, seemingly traveling in circles. And it nearly does, before returning to mature woods. The path continues looping through park woodlands before emerging in the developed center of the park. Complete the loop by cutting through the developed facilities to return to the trailhead.

Miles and Directions

0.0 Start from the asphalt pathway between the picnic shelter to your left and the restrooms to your right. Walk north just a few feet to enter woodland and cross a horse trail. Just

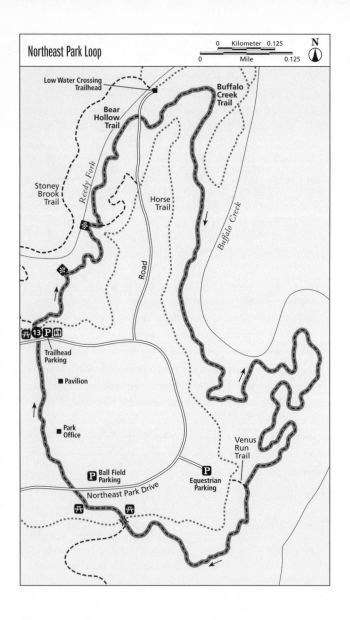

Northeast Park Loop

N

0   Kilometer   0.125
0   Mile   0.125

Low Water Crossing Trailhead

Buffalo Creek Trail

Bear Hollow Trail

Stoney Brook Trail

Reedy Fork

Horse Trail

Road

Buffalo Creek

13 P

Trailhead Parking

Pavilion

Park Office

P Ball Field Parking

P Equestrian Parking

Northeast Park Drive

Venus Run Trail

a few feet ahead reach the Reedy Overlook Trail. Turn right and join a natural-surface path under pines.

0.1 Reach a wooden platform overlooking Reedy Fork. Continue winding along the edge of a bluff, only to find a crease that leads down to bottomland.

0.2 Reach a second wooden platform overlooking Reedy Fork. This one is much closer to the water. Cross a wooden bridge, then come near a horse trail. Stay left, joining the Bear Hollow Trail as it cruises flats alongside Reedy Fork.

0.4 Reach the Low Water Crossing trailhead and access road. The parking area has a shaded table, good for picnicking. From here walk up the access road a short distance and then turn left, joining the Buffalo Creek Trail.

0.9 Turn away from Buffalo Creek and work around some large gullies.

1.1 Return to Buffalo Creek one last time before leaving the waterway and entering a young forest.

1.7 Intersect the Venus Run Trail just after entering mature hardwoods. Stay left, still on the Buffalo Creek Trail.

2.0 Cross a wooden bridge after coming near a horse trail. Shortly come alongside a clear field to your right with a picnic shelter in view. Leave the trail and walk toward the picnic shelter. Continue in the field, heading toward a second picnic shelter to your left. Cross Northeast Park Drive, joining an asphalt path heading north. Ball fields are to your left and a parking area is to your right.

2.1 Pass the park office on your right, then the park pool to your left.

2.3 Arrive back at the trailhead, completing the loop.

14 Guilford Mackintosh Lakeside Double Loop

This double loop hike takes place at Guilford Mackintosh Park, located on Lake Mackintosh, developed as a water source for Burlington. The elevation changes are sure to give exercise value to your shoreline trek. The main loop is nearly 3 miles in length, but you can cut it short to 1 mile, giving yourself ample time to enjoy other park facilities.

Distance: 2.8-mile double loop
Approximate hiking time: 1.5 to 2 hours
Difficulty: Moderate
Trail surface: Natural surfaces
Best season: March through May; September through November
Other trail users: Mountain bikers
Canine compatibility: Leashed dogs permitted
Fees and permits: No fees or permits required; trail users must sign in at trailhead.
Schedule: 8:00 a.m. to 6:00 p.m. in winter; 6:00 a.m. to 8:00 p.m. spring, summer and fall
Maps: USGS Gibsonville; Guilford Mackintosh Park & Marina
Trail contact: Burlington Parks and Recreation, 1345 NC 61 South, Whitsett 27377; (336) 449-2078; www.burlingtonnc.gov

Finding the trailhead: From exit 138 on I-40/I-85 between Greensboro and Burlington, follow NC 61 south for 0.5 mile; turn left into the park. Follow the main park road to dead-end at a parking area. Look for the sign stating trail entrance. GPS: N36 03.014' / W79 33.905'

The Hike

Burlington, one of the Triad communities, is growing fast. More water sources were obviously needed to sate the increasing population, so the authorities decided to create Lake Mackintosh. Later, Guilford Mackintosh Park was added along the shoreline. The new preserve is in great shape and offers a first-rate park experience. The trails are a lure for hikers and mountain bikers, but the park offers more than that.

The Big Alamance arm borders the park on two sides. Only self-propelled or electric motors are allowed in this arm of the lake, lending a quiet atmosphere to the park. A fishing pier, two bank-fishing areas, and a boat launch enhance the angling possibilities. The park rents boats, including paddleboats, should you want to tool around the lake. The park also has a quality picnic area, horseshoe pits, and a playground for kids.

Three loops make up the preserve's trail system. This hike includes two of them while taking the outermost trailway of all the loops to gain maximum mileage and scenery.

The hike leaves the well-kept developed facilities and curves along Lake Mackintosh. Hillside hardwoods, with a few cedars thrown in, shade the path. Beyond the Rock Bridge, the hike meanders into coves and out to peninsulas. The trailbed—as well as the surrounding woodlands—can be quite rocky. Note the white quartz outcrops as well.

Birders will be happy to know that multiple nesting boxes are located within sight of the trail. Three alluring stops are located along the loop. Two are picnic areas beside the lake; the final location features a gazebo overlooking the water. The hiking becomes easier once you leave the lake—the trail follows an old roadbed on a piney hilltop. Complete the second loop before reaching the trailhead.

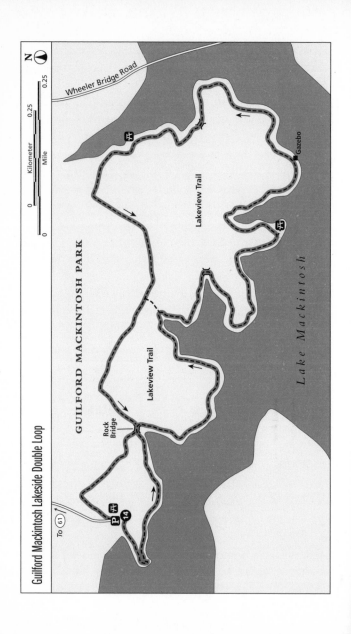

Guilford Mackintosh Lakeside Double Loop

Miles and Directions

0.0 Start from the parking area. Look for a sign stating TRAIL ENTRANCE and follow an asphalt path a short distance through a picnic area. Look for a dirt path leading left, beyond the trail sign-in board. Be sure to sign in.

0.3 Reach a four-way trail junction at the Rock Bridge, a small span stretching over an intermittent streambed. Cross the bridge and turn right, keeping Lake Mackintosh to your right.

0.5 Sweep onto a piney peninsula, meandering alongside Lake Mackintosh.

0.7 Reach a trail junction. Stay right, going for the full 2.8 miles. (**Option:** Turn left here for a 1.0-mile hike.)

0.8 Cross a wooden bridge over an intermittent streambed, well away from the lake.

1.0 Enjoy a southerly view into the Big Alamance Creek lake arm.

1.2 Reach a trail junction. A trail continues straight, descending to a picnic area at the lake's edge that's accessible by foot or boat. The main loop curves left (north) circling around a watery cove. Stay on the main loop.

1.5 A short spur trail leads right down to the water's edge and a gazebo overlooking Lake Mackintosh. The Wheeler Bridge is visible through the trees.

1.8 Cross a wooden bridge.

1.9 Reach a second picnic area with a table just after crossing another wooden bridge.

2.0 The loop makes a sharp left onto an old roadbed after entering a pine thicket. Enjoy the easy walking.

2.3 Reach the other end of the 1.0-mile loop shortcut trail to your left. Stay straight, descending.

2.5 Reach the stone bridge again. Cross the bridge and stay right this time, toward the trail exit, climbing a hill.

2.8 Arrive back at the parking area, completing the second loop.

15 Hagan-Stone Park: Chatfield Trail Loop

The Chatfield Trail loops around the entirety of Hagan-Stone Park. It begins as a lakeside singletrack path then travels along a babbling stream before making higher ground. It descends to cross one more stream before surmounting hills and returning to the trailhead. The natural environments range from pine thickets to hardwood bottoms to open meadows. A network of other paths intertwines with the Chatfield Trail and adds to the walking possibilities.

Distance: 3.4-mile loop
Approximate hiking time: 2 to 2.5 hours
Difficulty: Moderate; some hills
Trail surface: Natural-surface forest trail
Best season: March through May; September through November
Other trail users: Cross-country runners
Canine compatibility: Leashed dogs permitted
Fees and permits: No fees or permits required
Schedule: Open year-round 8:00 a.m. to sunset
Maps: USGS: Climax; Hagan-Stone Park; www.greens boro-nc.gov/NR/rdonlyres/ FF80D16A-B31D-41A8-9D3A-2546F30C5E3F/0/hsmap1.pdf
Trail contact: Hagan-Stone Park, 5920 Hagan-Stone Park Rd., Pleasant Garden 27313; (336) 674-0472; www.greensboro-nc .gov/departments/Parks/

Finding the trailhead: From exit 197 on I-40 on the south side of Greensboro, take US 421 South for 3.5 miles. Turn right onto Hagan-Stone Park Road and drive for 2.3 miles. Turn right into the park. Travel just a short distance and then turn left into the trailhead parking area, near Lake #2. GPS: N35 57.003' / W79 44.193'

The Hike

Hagan-Stone Park is located south of Greensboro in the town of Pleasant Garden. The 409-acre park was established in 1964, and the diverse facility offers hiking, camping, picnicking, swimming, fishing, and environmental education. The park is home to playgrounds, ball fields, and more. Park trails, including the Chatfield Trail, are used for cross-country running meets. You will note signs on your hike indicating directions for the 5K and 8K races. The park is also home to the Oak Grove Schoolhouse. This one-room school was built in the early 1900s. Schoolchildren of today come here and see what it was like to learn as they did a century ago.

The Chatfield Trail has many intersections, but all are signed. After leaving Lake #2, the trail traces the primary feeder stream of the lake. The rocky path works along the fern-lined brook, passing tributaries as you head farther upstream, including one small waterfall where the tributary meets a larger stream. The trail also passes the old Dogwood Trail, which is slated for abandonment. The forest transitions to oak with hickory and cedar as the Chatfield Trail nears the tent camping area.

The walking becomes pleasant as you cruise very level terrain. Beyond the Oak Grove School spur trail, the Chatfield Trail changes from singletrack to a wider path, as this section is used in cross-country meets. The trail continues meandering along the park boundary into tulip tree–dominated hardwood bottoms and piney hills. The moist bottoms can be good areas for wildflowers in spring. You may see "wolf trees" in the forest here. These are large old-growth trees with widespread branches. The widespread

Hagan-Stone Park: Chatfield Trail Loop

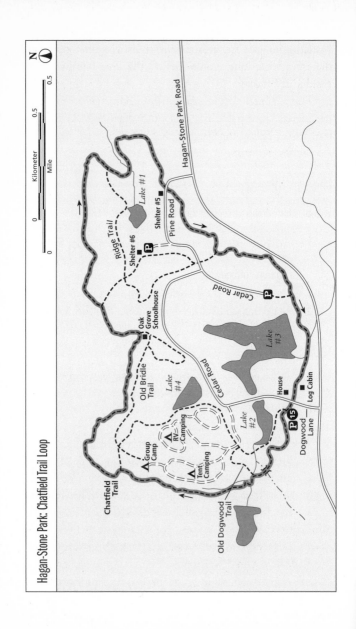

branches indicate the area around them was once open and the trees were lone wolves before the area became reforested as it is today.

The Chatfield Trail continues curving along the park perimeter, now paralleling Hagan-Stone Park Road. The trail passes below the dam of the park's biggest lake, Lake #3, before returning to the trailhead.

Miles and Directions

0.0 Start at the parking lot and turn left. Walk through the grass toward Lake #2 and pick up the Louise M. Chatfield Hiking Trail. Pass under a power line before entering woods and joining a very narrow track under lush woods. Begin tracing a stream northerly.

0.2 Cross a tributary of the stream you have been following.

0.3 The old Dogwood Trail heads right across a bridge. Stay straight as the Chatfield Trail crosses another tributary of the main stream.

0.7 Pass near the group camp.

0.8 The Draper Trail goes right. Stay left in flat woods as the Chatfield Trail begins to curve easterly.

1.0 Come alongside the Old Bridle Trail.

1.3 Intersect the Schoolhouse Trail. The trail leads right a short distance to the reconstructed Oak Grove Schoolhouse.

1.5 Stay left on the Chatfield Trail as a connector path leads right to the Ridge Trail and Picnic Shelter #6.

2.0 Reach a trail junction after turning south. The Chatfield Trail stays left, while the Ridge Trail veers right into pines and leads to Lake #1.

2.1 Bridge the stream flowing out of the Lake #1 dam. Soon traverse a gloomy pine/cedar thicket.

2.5 A spur trail leads right a short distance to Picnic Shelter #5. The Chatfield Trail keeps straight, passing beneath very tall pines.

2.7 Reach the other end of the Ridge Trail on your right. Keep rolling toward the trailhead.

3.0 A spur trail leads right to an alternate parking area. The Chatfield Trail stays left and drops into a wet area below the Lake #3 dam.

3.4 Reach the trailhead after the trail opens onto a grassy area and passes a rustic cabin.

16 Piedmont Environmental Center: Deep River Trail Loop

This hike combines the Bicentennial Greenway with the Deep River Trail, which travels along the shores of High Point Lake. The loop is located within the boundaries of the Piedmont Environmental Center and offers a fairly large wooded tract that preserves a wild slice of the Triad. Expect a decent workout while coursing through the lakeside hills.

Distance: 3.0-mile loop
Approximate hiking time: 1.5 to 2 hours
Difficulty: Moderate; some hills
Trail surface: Asphalt, natural surfaces
Best season: March through May; September through November
Other trail users: Bicyclists and joggers on Bicentennial Greenway
Canine compatibility: Leashed dogs permitted

Fees and permits: No fees or permits required
Schedule: Sunrise to sunset year-round; closed major holidays
Maps: USGS Guilford; Piedmont Environmental Center Trails; www.piedmontenvironmental .com/maps.htm
Trail contact: Piedmont Environmental Education Center, 1220 Penny Rd., High Point 27265; (336) 883-8531; www.piedmont environmental.com

Finding the trailhead: From exit 210 (High Point/PTI Airport) on I-40 near High Point, follow NC 68 south for 3.2 miles to Penny Road. Turn left onto Penny Road and follow it for 1 mile, then turn left onto East Fork Road and follow it toward the Jamestown Park and Golf Course. At 0.9 mile turn right into the stone gates of Jamestown Park and Golf Course. Follow the entrance road just a short distance before turning right and uphill into a parking area near Shelters

#1 and #2. The trail starts across East Fork Road from the entrance. GPS: N36 00.771' / W79 56.871'

The Hike

Piedmont Environmental Center provides not only an environmental study building but also preserved parcels in greater High Point. The tract through which this loop travels is known as the North Preserve. The Bicentennial Greenway makes its way through the North Preserve, following the old western leg of the Deep River Trail. Upon becoming the Bicentennial Greenway, the western leg was widened and paved over. The eastern leg of the Deep River Trail remains in its primitive singletrack state, leaving hikers with a mix of developed and primitive pathways.

Initially the loop travels through loblolly pine woods, with the evergreens rising high overhead. Interestingly, Piedmont Environmental Center aggressively uses fire to manage the forest here. This keeps the forest in its natural state, as this type of woodland needs occasional fires to keep it from evolving away from what it would normally be. An understory of beech and dogwood stands under the swaying trees, initially planted by the Civilian Conservation Corps (CCC) during the 1930s. Imagine the forest around you as eroded farmlands.

Roll through hilly terrain, speckled with resting benches, bridges over intermittent streambeds, and interpretive signs. The Bicentennial Greenway, which runs north–south, is marked in quarter-mile increments. It is slated to run 20 miles, connecting the cities of Greensboro and High Point.

Things change after you join the Deep River Trail. Your pathway changes to a narrow natural, rooty, and twisting tread that roughly parallels the shoreline of High Point Lake while winding in and out of rocky hollows. Occasional short paths lead to the water's edge. The final part of the hike rejoins the Bicentennial Greenway.

Miles and Directions

0.0   Start at the entrance of Jamestown Park and Golf Course. Cross East Fork Road and join an asphalt trail that heads just a short distance to meet the Bicentennial Greenway, also an asphalt track. Bear left (clockwise) onto the greenway.

0.2   Dip to a streambed.

0.4   Dip to a second streambed and then pass under a power line.

0.6   The Deep River Trail goes left as a dirt footpath. Stay right and descend toward old Sunnyvale Road. The path becomes gravel.

0.9   Reach a junction. Here the Bicentennial Greenway keeps straight. The Deep River Trail bears right as a footpath and immediately crosses a wetland on a wooden bridge. Join the Deep River Trail.

1.1   Come alongside High Point Lake.

1.3   Cross a streamlet on a bridge after briefly turning away from the lake. Return to the lake, now on a hillside cloaked in beech trees.

1.7   Cross a rocky stream where two watercourses meet and form a small cascade. Just ahead, the Hollis Rogers Pine Woods Trail goes right. Return to the lake before circling into another embayment.

2.2   Reach the other end of the Hollis Rogers Pine Woods Trail. Pass a large inscribed beech tree to the left of the trail and then circle around a large embayment.

2.5   Cross a bridge over one last streambed.

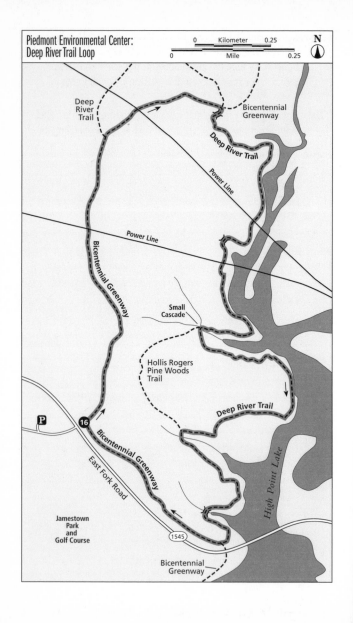

Piedmont Environmental Center:
Deep River Trail Loop

N

0   Kilometer   0.25
0   Mile   0.25

Deep River Trail

Bicentennial Greenway

Deep River Trail

Power Line

Power Line

Small Cascade

Hollis Rogers Pine Woods Trail

Bicentennial Greenway

Deep River Trail

High Point Lake

P

16

East Fork Road

Bicentennial Greenway

Jamestown Park and Golf Course

1545

Bicentennial Greenway

2.6 Reach a trail junction near East Fork Road. Turn right here, rejoining the asphalt Bicentennial Greenway and heading uphill away from the impoundment. The other end of the greenway heads to the Piedmont Environmental Center's South Preserve.

3.0 Reach a trail junction and complete your loop. Turn left and walk just a few feet to cross East Fork Road, completing the hike.

17 Piedmont Environmental Center: Lakeshore Double Loop

Much of this hike travels alongside High Point Lake, including the peninsula where the Raccoon Run Trail loops. The Lakeshore Trail intersects the other seven paths here, together forming a network that offers myriad environments to explore. Also, the Piedmont Environmental Center is a destination in its own right. Give yourself time to look and learn, even timing your visit with a naturalist program.

Distance: 2.7-mile double loop
Approximate hiking time: 1.5 to 2 hours
Difficulty: Moderate; some hills
Trail surface: Natural-surfaced forest trail
Best season: March through May; September through November
Other trail users: None
Canine compatibility: Leashed dogs permitted
Fees and permits: No fees or permits required
Schedule: Sunrise to sunset year-round; closed major holidays
Maps: USGS Guilford; Piedmont Environmental Center Trails; www.piedmontenvironmental .com/maps.htm
Trail contact: Piedmont Environmental Education Center, 1220 Penny Rd., High Point 27265; (336) 883-8531; www.piedmont environmental.com

Finding the trailhead: From Exit 210 on I-40 take NC 68 south for 3.2 miles to Penny Road. Turn left on Penny Road and follow it for 2.4 miles, then turn left into the Environmental Education Center. GPS: N36 00.193' / W79 57.254'

The Hike

Piedmont Environmental Education Center is more than just a nature preserve with hiking trails. It also is a learning and demonstration center, even down to the construction of the primary building, which uses all sorts of recycled materials as well as solar energy. The center occupies nearly 400 acres of land along High Point Lake and operates a 7,000-square-foot environmental education building. Naturalists are on hand to lead the year-round programs.

A big draw is the North Carolina mapscape—a 30- by 70-foot topographical relief map, complete with running rivers that is worth a visit in and of itself. Enjoy this and a stellar shoreline hike in hilly wooded terrain. Over 11 miles of trails occupy the preserve, including part of the Bicentennial Greenway. Beaver, deer, and many bird species can be found here.

The Lakeshore Loop leaves the visitor center and intersects many trails, each with highlights of its own. The Wildflower Trail is obviously popular in spring. See evergreens on the Pine Thickets Trail, while the Fiddlehead Trail has plenty of ferns.

The route described here begins curving toward High Point Lake. It picks up an old roadbed and then descends to meet the Dogwood Trail, which offers white blooms in spring. The trailside hickory-oak forest has an understory of young beech trees. Beech trees are easy to identify by their smooth gray bark. Also, young beech trees hold their dead leaves throughout the winter.

The Lakeshore Trail finally lives up to its name as it meanders alongside High Point Lake. Watery views range from obscured to first rate.

Your second loop is the Raccoon Run Trail. This makes its own circuit on a piney peninsula nearly surrounded by water. Your loop is nearing its end when you leave the peninsula and curve around a cove, intersecting more trails.

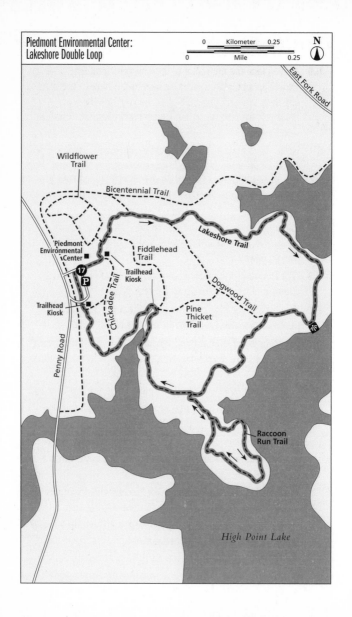

Piedmont Environmental Center:
Lakeshore Double Loop

0   Kilometer   0.25

0   Mile   0.25

N

Wildflower
Trail

Bicentennial Trail

Lakeshore Trail

East Fork Road

Piedmont
Environmental
Center

Fiddlehead
Trail

Trailhead
Kiosk

17

P

Chickadee Trail

Pine
Thicket
Trail

Dogwood Trail

Trailhead
Kiosk

Penny Road

Raccoon
Run Trail

High Point Lake

Miles and Directions

0.0 As you face the front door of the environmental education building, head right and cruise toward the back of the building then descend to a trail kiosk. As you face the kiosk, head left (clockwise) on the Lakeshore Trail, marked with a white dot.

0.1 Walk just a few feet before reaching a junction with the Wildflower Trail, which heads left. Wooden posts marked with the appropriate-color blaze indicate the intersections. Cross a streamlet then pass the Fiddlehead Trail. Your third junction veers left. It is an unnamed path that heads just a short distance down an old roadbed to meet the Bicentennial Greenway. Join the old roadbed, heading right, away from the greenway.

0.3 The Dogwood Trail continues on the old roadbed. The Lakeshore Trail heads left as a singletrack path.

0.9 The trail comes very near the shoreline and offers an excellent southward vista of High Point Lake to the dam.

1.1 Meet the south end of the Dogwood Trail in an old homesite with huge trees amid much brush. Stay left on the Lakeshore Trail.

1.4 Turn left onto the Raccoon Run Trail as it circles a peninsula.

2.0 Return to the Lakeshore Trail after completing the Raccoon Run loop. Turn left.

2.3 The Pine Thicket and Fiddlehead Trails head right. Stay on the Lakeshore Trail as it curves left around a cove. Cross a small stream.

2.5 The Chickadee Trail goes right. The Lakeshore Trail curves away from the lake and ascends for the parking area.

2.7 Reach the parking area after passing a trailhead kiosk and a spur trail leading to the Chickadee Trail.

18 Birkhead Wilderness Loop

This hike makes a loop through the crown jewel of the Uwharrie National Forest—Birkhead Mountains Wilderness. The circuit follows old roads from days gone by as well as narrow footpaths, passing over high ridges and along babbling streams of the ancient Uwharrie Mountains. On weekends you may see backpackers from the Triad toting their gear on overnight endeavors.

Distance: 6.9-mile loop
Approximate hiking time: 3.5 to 4.5 hours
Difficulty: More challenging due to hills and distance
Trail surface: Natural surfaces
Best season: March through May; September through November
Other trail users: None
Canine compatibility: Leashed dogs permitted
Fees and permits: No fees or permits required
Schedule: Open year-round
Maps: USGS Badin; Birkhead Mountains Wilderness; www .cs.unca.edu/nfsnc/recreation/ uwharrie/birkhead_mountains_ wilderness_info%20Map.htm
Trail contact: Uwharrie National Forest, 789 NC 24/27 East, Troy 27371; (910) 576-6391; www .cs.unca.edu/nfsnc/recreation/ uwharrie

Finding the trailhead: From the intersection of US 220 and US 64 in Asheboro, take US 64 west for 0.2 mile to NC 49. Follow NC 49 south for 6 miles and to turn right onto Science Hill Road (The left turn at this intersection is Tot Hill Farm Road). Follow Science Hill Road for 0.2 mile to Lassiter Mill Road. Turn left onto Lassiter Mill Road. Do not turn left into the signed Thornburg trailhead of Birkhead Mountain Wilderness at 2.7 miles. Instead drive a total of 5.6 miles on Lassiter Mill Road to the second signed turn into the Birkhead Mountains Wilderness. Turn left on this gravel road at 5.6 miles and follow it for 0.6 mile to dead-end at the trailhead. GPS: N35 35.401' / W79 56.920'

The Hike

The Birkhead Mountains Wilderness was established in 1984. Set at the northern end of North Carolina's oldest mountains—the Uwharries—the area is characterized by long wooded ridges divided by small, clear streams. Though the mountains do not top 1,000 feet at their highest points, they do feature surprisingly hilly terrain in the nearly 5,000-acre preserve.

Long before it was managed as a wilderness, the area was farmed and homesteaded, mined for gold, and cut over for timber. These days it is a destination enabling Triad residents to taste the back of beyond.

On this hike you will feel a sense of wilderness, but you'll also see the relics of man, including old roadbeds, homesites, rock walls, and even an erect chimney beside the trail. You will also pass the Christopher Bingham plantation site. In 1780 Bingham came to what was then the West and cultivated the Birkheads. Look for piles of stones and leveled land.

The trails are all natural surface, but unlike in some designated wildernesses, they are well marked with blazes and signage at intersections. Oak trees dominate the ridgelines, and other hardwoods border the streams. Mountain laurel and holly are found in abundance here. Pines thrive throughout the Birkheads. Quartz and other rocks are found along and on the trail, erosion-resistant relics of these once high mountains.

Miles and Directions

0.0 Start at the parking area. Take the trail heading north, the Robbins Branch Trail, traveling an old roadbed shaded by ridgetop woodlands. Roll over eroded soil vehicle berms.

0.3 Reach an intersection. Your return route, the Hannah's Creek Trail, heads right. Stay left (clockwise), still on the Robbins Branch Trail, rising through thick forest.

0.9 Note a tree to the right of the trail. It grows vertically then horizontally and then vertically again, forming a resting seat. In winter, views of the surrounding lands open to your east and west.

1.6 Reach a trail junction after descending from a high point. Here a trail leads left to the Thornburg trailhead. Turn right, descending toward Robbins Branch, to shortly pass an old rock wall on trail left.

1.9 Rock-hop Robbins Branch. Turn upstream.

2.0 Cross Robbins Branch twice in succession. Then cross it a fourth time.

2.7 Leave Robbins Branch; curve easterly and ascend.

3.1 Reach the ridgecrest and the Birkhead Trail. Turn right here, southbound.

3.5 Top out at 900 feet and reach Camp 5 and a large fireplace on the trail right. A yellow-blazed water access trail leads east to North Prong Hannah's Creek. The trail undulates among rock outcrops.

5.1 Reach the Christopher Bingham plantation site after dropping off the ridgeline.

5.2 Intersect the Hannah's Creek Trail. The Birkhead Trail continues straight. Turn right onto the Hannah's Creek Trail, rolling through hills.

5.4 Cross a tributary of Hannah's Creek. Rise to reach an erect double hearth chimney, the remains of a settler's homesite.

5.8 Cross another tributary of Hannah's Creek.

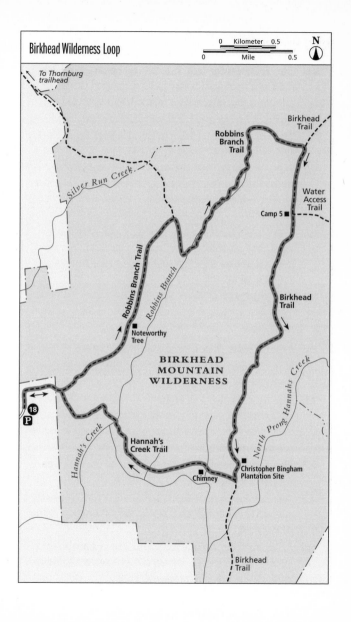

Birkhead Wilderness Loop

Kilometer
0   0.5
0   0.5
Mile

N

To Thornburg
trailhead

Silver Run Creek

Robbins
Branch Trail

Birkhead
Trail

Water
Access
Trail

Camp 5

Robbins Branch Trail

Robbins Branch

Birkhead
Trail

Noteworthy
Tree

BIRKHEAD
MOUNTAIN
WILDERNESS

North Prong Hannah's Creek

18
P

Hannah's Creek

Hannah's
Creek Trail

Chimney

Christopher Bingham
Plantation Site

Birkhead
Trail

6.2 Cross Robbins Branch after passing a settler's stone fence. Climb.

6.3 Pass an interesting stone outcrop that resembles a backbone.

6.6 Intersect the Robbins Branch Trail. You have now completed your loop. Turn left and backtrack to the trailhead.

6.9 Reach the trailhead, completing the wilderness hike.

19 Badin Lake Loop

This hike traverses along the shoreline of Badin Lake and through rugged hills of the Uwharrie National Forest in Montgomery County. You will have trouble keeping your eyes off the scenic lake views while watching your footing on rocky terrain. The undulating landscape has plenty of ups and downs, especially compared to other Piedmont destinations, so be prepared.

Distance: 5.5-mile loop
Approximate hiking time: 2.5 to 3 hours
Difficulty: More challenging due to hills and distance
Trail surface: Natural surfaces, a short stretch of asphalt
Best season: March through May; September through November
Other trail users: Bicyclists
Canine compatibility: Leashed dogs permitted

Fees and permits: No fees or permits required
Schedule: Open year-round
Maps: USGS Badin; Badin Lake Hiking Trail Map; www.cs.unca .edu/nfsnc/recreation/uwharrie/ badin_lake_trail_map.pdf
Trail contact: Uwharrie National Forest, 789 NC 24/27 East, Troy 27371; (910) 576-6391; www .cs.unca.edu/nfsnc/recreation/ uwharrie

Finding the trailhead: From the intersection of NC 49 and NC 109 south of High Point and southwest of Asheboro, travel for 8.8 miles south on NC 109 to Old Thayer Mill Road. Turn right onto Old Thayer Mill Road and follow it for 1.6 miles to McLeans Creek Road (FR 544). Turn right onto McLeans Creek Road and follow it for 1.7 miles to reach Badin Lake Road (FR 597). Turn right onto Badin Lake Road, aiming for Kings Mountain Point. At 0.2 mile veer left onto FR 597A. Follow FR 597A for 0.5 mile to reach an intersection. Go straight on Group Camp Road (FR 6551) to dead-end at 0.8 mile, reaching the Kings Mountain Point Picnic Area. GPS: N36 05.732' / W80 11.561'

The Hike

Kings Mountain Point Recreation Area—the hike's starting location—has been renovated. The site offers restrooms, picnic facilities, a small nature trail, and fishing platforms. A campground host is located on-site and makes for a good jumping-off point. The trail passes two nice campgrounds, Badin Lake and Arrowhead. They may tempt you to add an overnight campout to your Uwharrie National Forest adventure.

Leaves, rocks, and roots compose the natural-surface trail. Note the abundance of exposed milky-white quartz. Pine-oak woods with sweet gum tower over holly and dogwood. White blazes mark the path. Expect to step over occasional fallen trees.

The trail crosses numerous intermittent streambeds and others flowing full-time as it cruises along the shoreline of Badin Lake. Most of these streams can be easily rock-hopped, yet some places will be marshy or mucky, especially during winter and spring. Look for duck boxes placed at the water's edge. You are walking along the Beaverdam Creek arm of Badin Lake. The trail loops Badin Lake Campground between the campsites and the shoreline. The sites are so close to the trail, you may beg a hotdog if the campers are cooking.

The path temporarily leaves Badin Lake at Cove Boat Ramp, passing Arrowhead Campground and its mini trail system. From here the path winds through wooded piney hills and hardwood hollows before returning to the lake. Here you will cruise the shoreline again, reaching a peninsula's northern tip. Views are plentiful. The trail passes through arguably the steepest and most rugged terrain of the hike before reaching Kings Mountain Point.

Miles and Directions

0.0 Start at the parking area. As you look out toward the tip of Kings Mountain Point, the hiking trail leaves left from the upper part of the parking area. Travel south then east, counterclockwise, toward Badin Lake Campground on a single-track path passing amid shaded picnic tables.

0.2 After curving around an embayment, you can look north to Kings Mountain Point. Note the lakeside clearings used by bank anglers.

0.5 Step over an intermittent stream just before beginning your curve around Badin Lake Campground.

1.1 Reach a point and good lake vista.

1.7 Pass through a particularly rocky section of trail while circling a cove.

2.1 Reach Cove Boat Ramp. Walk on pavement toward the restroom, then veer left and look for steps leading uphill to the trail's resumption.

2.2 Reach a junction near Arrowhead Campground. Keep straight, joining a paved path. The paved path going left loops around the far side of the campground. Shortly pass a spur path leading left to the campground restrooms. Stay right.

2.4 Cross the campground entrance road.

2.5 Reach the far end of the Arrowhead Campground loop trail. Keep straight, now on a natural-surface trail that curves north.

2.8 Reach a hilltop in a young forest; shortly drop to cross an old forest road.

3.0 Cross the green-blazed Lake Horse Trail.

3.1 Cross the Lake Horse Trail a second time. Circle an old clearing.

3.3 Cross FR 597A. Work through some steep hills.

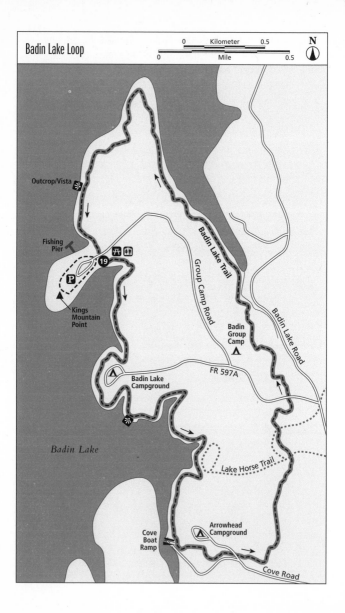

Badin Lake Loop

0   Kilometer   0.5
0   Mile   0.5

N

Outcrop/Vista

Fishing Pier

19

P

Kings Mountain Point

Badin Lake Trail

Group Camp Road

Badin Group Camp

FR 597A

Badin Lake Road

Badin Lake Campground

Badin Lake

Lake Horse Trail

Arrowhead Campground

Cove Boat Ramp

Cove Road

3.7 Come alongside the largest creek of the hike. Private property is located on the other side. Shortly reach Badin Lake again. Houses are located on the far side of the embayment.

4.7 Reach the northern tip of the peninsula you are following. Turn south toward Kings Mountain Point on steep and rocky terrain. Bisect several rocky gullies.

5.2 Pass an open rock outcrop with a superlative lake vista.

5.5 Arrive at Kings Mountain Point, completing the hike.

20 Boone's Cave Loop

This hike along the banks of the Yadkin River makes a loop in thick woods, first visiting a state-record cottonwood tree before coming to the prize—Boone's Cave. Daniel Boone and family purportedly spent time under this rock shelter as a respite from the weather and protection from Indians.

Distance: 1.8-mile loop with spur

Approximate hiking time: 1 to 1.5 hours

Difficulty: Moderate, steep hills

Trail surface: Natural surfaces, gravel

Best season: March through May; September through November

Other trail users: None

Canine compatibility: Leashed dogs permitted

Fees and permits: No fees or permits required

Schedule: 8:00 a.m. to 5:30 p.m. in winter; 8:00 a.m. to 8:00 p.m. in summer; open Sunday at 1:00 p.m.

Maps: USGS Churchland; Boone's Cave Park; www.visit davidsoncounty.com/images/ PDF/BCP%20brochure.pdf

Trail contact: Davidson County Parks & Recreation, P.O. Box 1067, Lexington 27292; (336) 242-2285; www.co.davidson.nc .us/leisure/BoonesCavePark

Finding the trailhead: From the intersection of US 52 and US 64 on the west side of Lexington, take US 64 west toward Mocksville. Stay on US 64 for 2.9 miles to reach NC 150. Follow NC 150 west toward Salisbury and travel 7.6 miles to Boone's Cave Road. Turn right onto Boone's Cave Road and follow it for 3.6 miles to dead-end at the park. Continue a little farther and park at the park ranger cabin. GPS: N35 47.874' / W80 27.875'

The Hike

Boone's Cave Park is a one-hundred-acre preserve on the southeast shore of the Yadkin River. Half the park acreage is a designated National Heritage Site, as the park is home to nearly fifty Tar Heel State native wildflowers. A picnic shelter is located on a high bluff where you can gain an extensive sweep of the Yadkin.

Of course the park is best known as being home to Boone's Cave. It has been handed down for generations that Daniel and his family used the cave when they moved down here from Pennsylvania. Many other place-names in Davidson County bear the Boone moniker. Though there is no concrete evidence that they used the cave, Daniel and his family did settle the Yadkin Valley, and Daniel certainly passed this way while hunting.

Your hike also leads to Baptism Rock, located just below the cave. Here an open outcrop extends to the water. Local churches have used this as a ceremonial dunking spot for christenings. The park is also home to the state-record eastern cottonwood tree. A spur trail leads to the base of the giant.

This special swath of the Piedmont has been recognized for decades—the park was first developed in 1909. The cabin foundation of the 1940s park caretaker still stands. There is 1750s-era reconstructed log cabin on the site that is only accessible by trail.

The hike itself makes a loop from the park entrance down a hollow to the Yadkin. Once along the riverbanks the trail travels to the three aforementioned outstanding shoreline features before traveling up a separate hollow to reach the trailhead.

Boone's Cave is smaller and lower than you might imagine. Should you enter the cave, it will be cool in summer and warm in winter. Interpretive signage placed throughout the loop enhances your hike. Stay tuned for updates, as more foot trails are being added to the park.

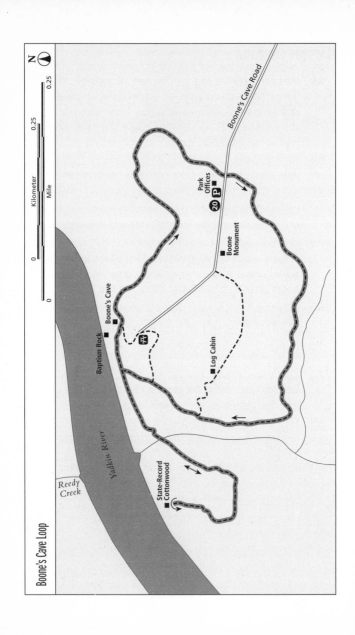

Boone's Cave Loop

Miles and Directions

0.0 Start at the parking area near the park ranger cabin. Cross the park entrance road and join a gravel track, descending sharply down to a steep-sided hollow. Come alongside a streambed and begin meandering toward the Yadkin River. Thick hardwoods shade the track.

0.4 Open onto a tree-covered flat. Steep bluffs stand on your right. The Yadkin River lies to your left through the trees.

0.5 Reach a trail junction. Steps lead right and uphill to the reconstructed 1750s-era cabin. Shortly reach another trail junction. A steep trail leads right to the picnic shelter.

0.6 Reach another trail junction. A spur trail on the left leads out and back, following the Yadkin River downstream to the North Carolina state-record eastern cottonwood tree. The tree is old enough that Daniel might have laid eyes on it.

0.9 After meandering through brushy bottoms, reach the record tree. Backtrack.

1.2 Return to the trail junction you were at earlier. This time turn left to head upstream, with the Yadkin River to your left.

1.3 Shortly pass Baptism Rock on your left, then Boone's Cave. Wooden steps lead to the picnic shelter above. Turn away from the river, ascending a hollow.

1.8 Level out after ascending the hollow, then make a short descent to reach the park ranger cabin, completing the loop.

About the Author

Johnny Molloy is a writer and adventurer with an economics degree from the University of Tennessee. He has become skilled in a variety of outdoor environments and written over three dozen books, including hiking, camping, paddling, and comprehensive regional guidebooks as well as true outdoor adventure books. Molloy has also written numerous articles for magazines, Web sites, and blogs. He resides in Johnson City, Tennessee. For the latest on Molloy's pursuits and work, please visit www.johnnymolloy.com.